Hippie Diary

STEPHEN M. CATCHPOLE

ISBN-13: 978-87-995799-0-7

DEDICATION

To all those who took that journey and went on the road.

CONTENTS

ACKNOWLEDGMENTS

Cover photographs by Barry Wood.

Editing by Anni Lockl.

Thanks to everyone who gave input.

i

1. Introduction

This document is a diary that I kept on what is now commonly known as a 'Road Trip'. Back then it was known as dropping out or going 'On the Road'. I went with a friend called Barry who was part of an inner circle of four friends: Barry, Pip, Paddy and me. Pip and I had been friends since about the age of six. He came from a middle class family that was living on the council estate where I lived while they saved for a house. We remained friends after he moved and through him I got to know Barry and Paddy.

Barry and Paddy were about one year older than us but not what you would call in today's terms wiser. We all got loaded together and hung out and went to concerts and festivals. We lived in holes in the ground called Camberley and Frimley. I am sure they are nice towns now but back then they were real dumps where absolutely nothing was going on for young people. We used to meet on Saturday afternoons, smoke a joint in the park and Paddy would read out loud the serialized edition of 'Fear and loathing in Las Vegas' from Rolling Stone Magazine. Occasionally we would go to London to buy records, like Country Joe and the Fish and Roy Harper. Paddy was the authority on music and always found the best tracks that hit you when you were high. In the hole we lived in it was hard to find good records. Legend had it that the couple who owned the record shop by the Odeon owned the two or four track tape machine that *'The Who'* had made their first singles on. I remember seeing it in the corner, it looked very usual, just a tape deck. There was also a record shop in Camberley High Street that had mainstream stuff. The place we hung out was at the other end of town across the street from the betting shop. We would be browsing through the selection surrounded by posters of the new Nick Drake album 'Five Leaves Left' and some old Irish guy would come in and ask "Excuse me lads, what is the latest Beatles album?" and we would pass him 'Abbey Road'.

The only known person to escape from that hole was Nick Tesco who formed a band called the 'The Members' in 1976. Nicky was a regular Jack the Lad. I was not really a close friend but I went by his place a few times and we got high. He always seemed to me to shuffle around in some bundle of joy always with a happy smirk. I remember vividly him coming into a pub one evening in 1972 with Ford T (I shit you not) parked outside. He had bought it for a few quid that was cheaper than a train to Liverpool where he was going to study at that time. Somehow I got dragged into this or tagged along. We had some dope and at some time past London people started to get drowsy in the back as the exhaust pipe was leaking. We tied some rags around it and carried on *Job well done!* That was until flames started gushing out from under the car. We stopped at a petrol station and got some kind of repair kit. As far as I remember Nick just parked the car on a street in

Liverpool and walked away. I think I hung around for a couple of days then went back to Camberley. That's how things were in those days. In 2013, I asked Nicky if he could remember the incident and he replied from his holiday in France: *"only just got online! That's exactly right what a f..king laugh. Also we had to call a doctor because we all turned blue and got carbon monoxide poisoning!"* Confirmation from the man of few words Nick Tesco.

(Nick says of Camberely) *"I've got really great memories of the people I hung out with, the people I partied with, but the place itself was just this white hate filled violent comfort zone / I grew to despise its small town suburban mindset, its racism and general fear of otherness. So when I was offered a ticket to Canada I jumped on it"*

That is how it was back then, friends came and went. Basically, anyone who got the chance to leave took it. One day Pip just up and left and went to London. We were talking one day and he asked me if I had any money, I told him I had about twenty quid savings and he said "If I had twenty quid, I'd leave this place, do you want to buy my record player and some records?" In that way I helped finance his escape by buying his records and his Dansette record player. I don't remember how much I paid but it would not have been all my savings. I was grilled by his mum later *"What I would like to know is where he got the money from and who bought his record player?" Beats me!* Was the only reply I could think of. Pip and I were listening to Neil Young all the time back then and *'Sugar Mountain'* comes to mind whenever I think about that time. A lot of the songs like Dylan's *"It's All over Now Baby Blue"* were basically saying it was time to leave home and the past would not follow you when you moved on.

I lived on the Old Dean Council Estate. I belonged to what was known as *'The London Overflow'* people from London who had been relocated to council estates outside London. My upbringing was lower working class. No books in the house, no newspapers except *'News of the World'* on Sundays. No fridge, no central heating, no hot water unless the immersion heater was plugged in. That usually happened on Friday when the whole family shared one lot of bath water. I was encouraged to leave school as soon as possible to contribute to the household rent. I slept on a mattress on the floor in an upstairs box room with no furniture or curtains. All the food was from tins, canned meat and canned vegetables. Nothing was ever fresh, not even cheese. It was always cheese spread wrapped in tinfoil. White sliced bread and condensed milk in the tea. Lunch was always a tin of Campbell's soup and bread.

I was working in a factory called *'Peppers of Woking'* on the Frimley Industrial Estate. I was 'real' working class me. You clocked in and clocked out. Spent your lunch break in the pub or

over in the park at Sandhurst Military College, feeding the ducks
by the lake. One of the few highlights in a day was if the boss's
mini - skirted secretary walked across the shop floor. Barry and
Paddy came from council estates in Frimley. To understand our
lives just look on YouTube at the opening scene[1] of '*Saturday
Night Sunday Morning*'. Every move Albert Finney made on that
factory floor I made, right down to washing my hands in the white
cooling oil. Like the character in the film I cycled to work and had
much the same prospects as he did. I left school at 14 in 1969
because I had my 15th birthday in July which was during the school
holidays. As I remember they had just put the school leaving age
up to 16 so I was in the last batch to get out. Thank God for that
because I could not have taken much more. Most of my teachers
in school were misfits left over from the Second World War and
we were being bought up as factory fodder. They were nasty
sadistic pieces of work and we were at their mercy. As an adult I
managed to go to England and drive by my old school. I pulled
over the car, walked over and pissed on it. A very feeble gesture I
know but Patton and Churchill peed in the Rhine so I thought the
act must have some class. I could not start an apprenticeship in
the factory right away, which is what my stepfather wanted for
me. So to pass the time until there was a vacancy I worked in the
butchers department of a supermarket called '*Gateways*' in

---

[1] http://www.youtube.com/watch?v=zJAeb0wiQjA

Camberley High Street. I hung out with different groups of friends. Went to London on days off with my Smoothie mates and visited strip clubs in Soho *"you boys 18?"* A deep voice answered, *"Yes sir"*. I often went to London on odd days with my mate Dave. He remembers we always missed the last bus and had to run across to Waterloo train station. We were always running me and Dave, for buses and trains (or from Skinheads). Going up to London was special. London always had a great feeling about it and still does. For young people nothing was happening in Camberley. Apart from one bloody coffee bar in the High Street called 'Gallinis' nothing was open downtown after the pub closed. A concert now and then at Farnborough Technical College and that was it. I went to a Grand Funk Railroad concert in Hyde Park with Barry, Paddy and Pip who were more 'Hip'. It was on that trip they dissuaded me from joining the RAF which is something I was planning to do. They also went to the Isle of Wight festival and saw Dylan and Hendrix and loads of others. I did not go with them because I thought it would be too messy with all the drugs and mud and stuff. How I regret that now. Instead I went for a boat trip round the Isle of Wight with Ron who worked in the butcher shop. He came from Portsmouth and we worked on his Dory down there at week-ends. Putting a cabin on it and making a small sail. I mention buying him some pipe tobacco in the diary.

As I said Barry and Paddy were a couple of years older than me and Pip. That did not mean very much, we all worked and we all went to the pub on Friday nights. But it meant that they had been planning to go 'on the road' for a couple of years. They would both save their money and be all set to leave, then Paddy would buy some dope with the intention of selling some to cover the expenses and smoke the rest. Unfortunately for a few years in a row, Paddy smoked more than he sold. This meant that more than once they had to cancel the trip. That was how I ended up going instead of Paddy.

One of the things I learned from my rotten working class upbringing was saving. You spend your money but you always put some aside. It seems funny now but Harold Macmillan had to introduce Premium Bonds in 1956 to encourage working people to save in the post war period. Like in the opening sequence in Saturday Night Sunday Morning, the charge hand in the factory comes round with envelopes with your wages in. Money was not transferred to bank accounts. As a factory boy you went home, gave your mum half for rent, then spent the rest or went to the bank and put some in your savings account. I had saved up about a fifty quid (£50) which is about £560 in today's money. Barry was talking in the pub one night about how he wanted to go on the road and I was game. At the time I was half way through my apprenticeship at the factory and gave in my notice. They tried to dissuade me with lectures about *"think about your future, wait till you are finished in two years then travel".* But I had seen class mates at Farnborough Technical College who were under 20 years old and had kids. They were really stitched up. Their fate was sealed and I just had to walk away from what I saw as a dead-end life of work in a factory and the security that came with it. I wanted to take the road of uncertainty. I did not really know what I wanted but I knew what I did not want and that was the soul destroying life I had in Camberley. How long would we be gone? For a month or for a year, we had no definite plans. As Barry later pointed out to me, we did not even have return tickets.

I must have thought at the time that the trip was something special and worth making some kind of record of because I kept this small journal. Barry was interested in photography and took a good quality camera. These are my notes exactly as I made them, a snapshot of the time, illustrating the zeitgeist? (I have also given some footnote explanations to some events). Perhaps, it is always hard looking back at ones youth. Now everything seems to be instant. You Google something (like premium bonds) and get an instant answer. When I think about records in the charts that were hits during the 1960's, I think they must have happened over a long period of time. When I look them up on Wikipedia months or weeks passed between them not years!!! Music was one of the key elements of that era and new stuff was coming out all the time. Barry and I loved the Stones 'Exile on Main Street'and many

Americans I met on the road got homesick when they heard Neil Young's 'Harvest'.

The only extra thing I have added to these notes (apart from a few name changes of people who I have not been able to contact) is an extract from a letter I got in Venice, Italy. It was from an American girl who I met at the Grand Funk Railroad Hyde Park Concert on July 3rd 1971. She was coming back to Europe and wanted to meet up. As the letter came via the UK she had already left when I received it. Back then there were no mobiles or internet. People's paths crossed or they connected. We did not connect and she ended up going to Jamaica anyway, so she and I travelled different roads. I include the piece of her letter because it shows the feeling of the times. What she felt many people like me and Barry felt and that was why we left. Some people went and some people stayed home. All through the sixties people had been turning on and 'going on the road'. For people like me, 1972 is very much part of the sixties phenomena because nothing really happened in the sixties before the Beatles came along in 1963. Ten years later in 1973 the Vietnam War that had played such a huge role during the sixties ended thereby closing the era.

Finally one should always remember there is no formula how to live your life.

You can always change the direction your life is taking if you really want to.

Your youth is one of the most precious times on your journey through life so don't waste it doing something you hate.

I do not recommend any of the things I did as a solution to anything.

I only hope some people can recognize and identify with some of the things I wrote down back then.

Remember this was 40 years ago and neither Barry nor I condone the use of drugs in any form or the excessive use of alcohol.

This should be seen purely as a historical document from that time.

A record of the journey I made in my youth.

2. Road Trip with Barry Wood (part one)

This is a copy of a diary I kept on a Road Trip with Barry Wood from Frimley through Europe in 1972. It was written in a blue paperback school notebook: item 2 / B/ 7 Note Book 7x4½, 60 pages dated 1968. Surrey County Council. On the front cover I had written: 'April, May, Julio'. 'Birthday' and 'Pension, US Consulate, American Express'. On the back I have written 'Photomax', '2 o'clock' and 'P. Letter, Banks'. Inside the back cover it says "I'll be gone Sunday"

The diary starts Sunday, but there is no date. I can see from my Youth Hostel card we checked into the Hostel in Troyes the 28th of March. Barry confirmed this by telling me he told his Dad we were going grape picking! Showing how little people in the UK knew about the climate on the Continent. Barry's Dad Sid is a great bloke and he drove us down to Southampton. I have unclear recollections about the route we took. I always thought we started by going to Troyes but according to the diary we headed straight for Paris and got there in three lifts. The first day written is Sunday then Monday, Tuesday. In the opening text I have written Wednesday and Thursday. According to the 1972 calendar the 28th of March was a Tuesday. This means we probably left the UK on Sunday 19th March 1972. I have copied the document exactly as it was written, including some spelling mistakes. Stephen M. Catchpole 18th November 2012

SUNDAY - Got to Southampton at 4.30. Left for Le - Harve at
11.30. MONDAY Arrived at Le – Harve (?) had food bought 200
fags. Made for Paris done it in 3 lifts. Sent two post card one to
mum one to Julie who I constantly think of. From Paris central
made for a Youth Hostel by Metro, the people are very friendly
and helpful. Waited for the Hostel to open met 2 French
Canadians and one yank from San Diego. 14f. a night too much.
Split with the yank into central Paris again found a hostel for 12f.
TUESDAY Had breakfast, ripped off some bread. Re pack our gear.
Sent 2 cards one to Jeanie one to Pete and John.
Tried to phone Alien not in. Now sitting by Notre - Dam.
After eating our normal diet of bread and honey.

Saw the Notre – Dam. Then the Eiffel Tower. Met a South African
guy who called Paris "The Shit". Headed for Aliens on the way had
a bottle of wine and said "South man" off we went. Got a lift out
of Paris by a drunk who said we could sleep at his flat.
WEDNESDAY. Went South got a lift by a really nice teacher who
invited us to dinner. Lamb, Fish, Peas, Bread cheese, Wine, Beer,
Cognac, Homemade wine, cigars, cigarettes, pattie. From then on
the hitching was bad for some reason Lorries never stop. Slept in
a bus shelter very cold. Thursday. Changed route at Memours
went to Sene saw the church the Architecture much the same as

Notre – Dam. Now heading for Troyes where there is a concert tomorrow for 3 days.

Slept in garage the people were very friendly and bought us coffee in the morning. I was ill during the night due to a bottle of wine a nice old lady had given us. My sleeping bag is now no good! Got a lift to Troyes I was still feeling ill and dizzy. But felt better after a yogurt. Got to the Hostel 4 francs a night feeling exhausted so booked for three. Met two nice French girls who had come for the concert, groups were Led Zep. Who, TYA, but it was cancelled, the girls names were Martine & Rewjean. They gave us food and dope they were both pretty and 17 years old.

(Saturday 1st April) after three days of really great time and good company and carving Julie's name on walls. We headed for the South coast got a lift 50km from Lyon by two ladies who bought us coke and crisps. Slept in a bus shelter. In the morning a lift to Lyon by a student. Then we met a nice guy from Toulon who had been living on the Spanish boarder he gave us chocolate. Also a guy from GB heading home from Morocco, we nearly headed there after speaking with him. Then got a lift to Valance by a soldier we're half way there now. We met a girl (French) coming home from Tunisia with a guy she was very friendly and really nice and was the splitting image of Julie also we met an old guy 4 Yankees 2 were nice and a load of French hippies heading for

Manheim to a concert; Pink Floyd, Byrds. The old guy[2] bought us all 2 meals really nice bloke. Slept by the motorway entrance with them. In the morning got a lift by a great young couple who took us all the way to Marseille, then to top that they picked us up later and took us to Cassis where we met 2 girls travelling in a car. They gave us food and dope also a black dosser who showed us a great place to sleep where we got stoned, lit a fire and got paranoid. Next day they brought us here, a deserted beach by a naval base. We have been here 4 nights, they left after two. Have written to mum and Julie giving an address, really looking forward to hearing from them. Have made friends yesterday with eight of the village girls only 14 but good company and they bring us food. Before the girls left in the car they bought us sausage and chips and wine total 26f.about 2 quid.

Left 30th April hitched to Saint Tropez sent a letter to Julie got a

---

[2] This 'Old Guy' (probably younger than I am now) was heading for Laos. In the beginning Barry and I could not understand what he was saying Louse!! Louse!! Then he showed us on a map and we saw it was Laos, right down by Vietnam. I remember we said "you sure mate? You know there is a war on down there and they don't exactly love the French" who had been colonialists in that area. In a way, by buying meals for everyone he took on the role of looking out for us. We all thought he was nuts back then but looking back I can see he wasn't. He was just on an overland journey travelling as people had travelled for centuries sharing with fellow travelers whose paths he crossed. I hope he made it to Laos. He was a good bloke. These kinds of meetings were really inspiring. You are stranded somewhere in the sunshine and people gather, talking about where they are going or where they are coming from. They made you think anything was possible. Barry also said recently that he even thought we might have gone all the way to Katmandu. Now it is pretty commonplace to fly there but back then young people went overland either hiking or in 'Magic' buses.

lift about 2 miles. Stayed on a beach 4 nights and tonight 4th June. Tomorrow head for Nice if pos, wrote to Julie today. Been eating a lot lately been pissed quite often. Gave my harmonica[3] away and some other gear. We went into the bakers the other day and bought a loaf of bread and the lady gave us a big cake free. Woody's eye infection that he caught in the field has cleared up.

LA LOND

Stayed by a tree a few more nights. Then some rain came and we moved to some empty chalets. Stayed about a week, the girls bringing us grub and magazines. Then one morning at 7 o'clock two cops was hollering outside the window. Took us to the station searched our gear and threw us out on the road where we sat down and ate our porridge, that we made the night before.

Remember well the joy of getting two letters one from Lawrence one from Julie she really writes nice letters and some of the real her shows through which makes me glad. Stayed in a field a week the girls still bringing food to go with our diet of:
RICE, SEMULE, TABYOCA; COFFEE; PORRIDGE and bread and cheese. Left sadly behind the girls[4] who had come quite fond of

---

[3] I exchanged the harmonica with a French vagabond. For a Catholic medallion from French prison hostel. He had a cart and a dog. Barry says he was a bit of a nutter who also had a gun so we did not hang around long.

[4] I corresponded with one of them when I got back to England. She sent me the Michel Polnareff 45 'Holidays' and I sent her a Neil Young 45 'Down By the River' on Reprise with Cinnamon Girl alternate version on the B side. They

our company and a spade sailor called BEGGY, nice chap.

Got my last letter from Julie and left 3 days later.

FREJUS Hostel arrived 4th June and left June 5th – Walked here and stayed at the Youth Hostel. Ate and had hot coffee first cup for a week met the second English person had a a long chat met also two nice Canadians. Was told the hostel at Nice was OK and today will try and get there, paid 2f 50c + 2f extra for a sheet. The guy that runs the place was a creep and dogs kept us awake half the night. Raining hard so decided to stay two more nights till it wears off, met a GB guy called David gave him my needle cord shirt really nice guy, talked to him a lot about my problems.

WEDNESDAY _ Starting for Menton have split from Barry and we met in Nice walked 18km into the mountains its really beautiful. Got a lift to Cannes where I ate my sandwiches and a small plastic bottle of wine, I shall use the bottle for water, got a ride to Nice. Barry was in the hostel but it was full. Left for Menton with a yank who had just left Spain, got a lift off students to Menton, missed Monte Carlo slept outside the hostel, in the morning the yank was gone and to my amazement I still had my money, good guy.

(I can see in my Youth Hostel card it is stamped A.J. MENTON, 8 JUIN 1972). Went into the hostel met 2 Swedes went to the beach

---

used to sit together and sing 'Holidays' and I used to hum the opening to 'Down by the River' which seemed to fascinate them. One of them visited Barry many years later in the UK around the time he was getting married.

ate (they paid) swam went back. Barry arrived; we and the Swedes had a liter of rum and a bottle of coke. The owner of the hostel was very angry. I was sick 3 times, twice out the window and the third time I just leaned out of bed.

Slept outside Barry in. Sunbathed, ate, headed for Italia met 2 Krauts and wipped a big bag of oranges. Walked through the frontiers got a ride to San Remo slept out got soaking wet too tired to move. Got 2 rides and made it to the hostel Andora Marina met 2 people we saw in Frejus. Got 2 rides again went to a monastery but was deserted. Saw a fantastic graveyard of family crypts (The water at the monastery was the best I've tasted. Old Alleys).

Slept in the porch of a villa saw many fire flies. In the morning we climbed over the mountain and Barry went round the top was beautiful. Made it to Savona where we slept in a hut near a ruined castle now we are trying for Genova, hope there are letters from Julie.

WEDNESDAY – Got a ride all the way. Got lost from Barry in a Kasbah type market. Raining hard made my way to the Ostelle and slept in the shed out the back where I found blankets, ate my bread, fish, doughnuts and chocolates.

THURSDAY – Left my gear in the shed and went to town where I met two hippies on their way to a concert E.L.P. they were asking for money "Scuse, Chin Quanto Lire, De Panna". I tried and a guy gave me a 500 lire bill, drank 2 cartoons of milk and 1 doughnut. Went to a museum, all animals and visited 3 churches, bought a cake to go with bread and fish. And slept in the shed again.

FRIDAY – Packed my gear and now going to look for Barry. Barry was gone, met a yank called John, went to town, he'd lost $100, went to US Embassy and cop shop. Then went to Camogili, slept out after 2 liters of wine.

In the morning met 5 nice girls on vacation, had dinner, when we left they gave us gifts, one gave me a wrist band and beads, really nice people. A guy took a photo and just walked up and asked for my address. Got to Portofino, the yank got a hotel room, I got in round the back. Talked to some Germans and they bought a bottle of wine. Then we caught a bus (this yank) to Saint Margarette, went into a disco, not much good, had DJ's finished drink, got some more discos, name never paid 2,000 lire. I just play Greek. The next place we got thrown (coro) out but I threw a glass on the floor first. The next place we went in they were gonna throw the yank in the sea. He went for his knife, I went out and they grabbed me and searched me for a knife, then we were offered drinks. I ripped off a 500 lire tip and 40 fags and a lighter, everyone was friendly. I was pissed with 3 bottles of wine; this guy bought us Jack Daniels whiskey £1 a glass. He had a bottle of whiskey that cost £20. I got given a 10,000 lire bill and the guy who gave us a lift home gave me a 50,000 lire bill. It was 3.30 or 4 when we got in and slept till 12.00.

In the morning it was really nice to have music, the Stones 'Hot Rocks'. Will go to the disco tonight. But now I will post a card to Julie and maybe go to the hostel. Met two guys from Venosula, they gave us a lift from Portofino to St. Margreta where we booked into a pension (cheap hotel). Then went to Genoa. Got a letter from Julie and John was ripped off 2000 lire trying to score but we had a smoke. Went back to the Hotel and started replying to Julie while John bathed. Then the 2 South Yanks picked us up. 1 sandwich and coke 1000 lire, went round all the disco's, everywhere was dead, Sunday night I guess, ended up 1 Vodka and beer later in the same disco as last night, got bought a fillet steak and beer, bout £8 for both of us. Walked home and 5 in the morning, took a boat out, then got back, had a smoke and crashed till 12.30 next day.

MONDAY – Had a pkt. of biscuits for breakfast 180 lire. John had two sandwiches and a coke 900 lire. The hotel bill came to 5000 lire. Went to the bank found out I couldn't purchase cheques. Got a train, left our luggage at the station, 20 minutes 750 lire. John argued and the word F..K slipped out and the guy understood and leaped over the counter hollering. We settled it and paid.

John caught the train to Monte Carlo. I went back to Camogili and the 5 nice girls left my pack at their place. Stayed for tea, hung around till 1 o'clock then slept on the yanks air bed on the quayside.

TUESDAY – Woke up at 7 went to the girls place to sort out my gear. Went to Genoa, bought a brush and a skin water bottle, some guy gave me some smoke. Bought £32 of travelers cheques after a hassle. Got back quick to say goodbye to one of the girls. Then went to a cartoon movie, wow, in English. Then slept at Tony's flat after eating my fill of caramel pudding, like junket mm.

Woke up next morning at 11.30, went to the girls house to write to mum. Also I'll write to Julie.

Walked 2 km saw a church, made a knife for the girls. One of thems boyfriend who was anothers brother arrived, nice guy, got drafted. Found a place to crash with a French couple who had a tent. Tomorrow I will write Julie.

THURSDAY- Woke up went up a mountain in the morning, had a smoke. Read Julie's letters and decided to move for a while. Went back, had fried chicken for dinner said goodbye to the soldier. Had rice, egg, cheese mix, peas, meat, gravy, cake, wine, sausages and bread for tea. They sure have big meals. Wrote to Julie and mum, hope I wrote the right thing, in her own little way she's telling me to, turn on, tune in, drop out and do my own thing.

Tomorrow I'll leave with little equipment.

FRIDAY – (sent a card to JC[5] sayings don't write). Decided not to leave, then John arrives, he had met two US ballet dancer girls, Janet & Viki. Went to Genoa, had a smoke, drove around all night, crazy, had wine. The girls popped in at 4.30, had a smoke got no sleep, when they left, John did.

SATURDAY 24th July – Wrote to JC sending a purse and wrote mum also enclosing a purse. Got bothered by the cops 3 times, had to empty my pack on the last check.
John got the train South to where he hits Greece. Left me his air bed and 500 lire, good guy John, little fast with the money but OK. Today sent the purse to mum and Julie. Also my birthday today. And at 4.30[6] the girls bought me a meal as a treat but they didn't wake me, after 4 bottles of wine it would have been hard.

SUNDAY – Drove to Savona, went for a swim. The guy I found in the square split. Had a smoke, when Roberta went upstairs, 5 minutes later I went outside and heard 'Bules'[7] running. Got up at 2.30, went shopping. Rob bought a mirror blouse. Rob woke me up at 4, I'd been asleep a half hour, stayed up, went out and bought a Melody Maker and bread. The cops came and told me to move the VW van. Vic came back 2 days late, bought me an ice

---

[5] JC and JULIE is the same person.
[6] They worked in a club and always got off at 4.30 in the morning.
[7] This word is not clear , might be someone's name

cream, cake, melon, pizza, soda, biscuits. I got FREE LOVE CASSETTE. They got N.Y. HARVEST, went to their room and played them. Had tea there. 5 o'clock, they woke me and said we're going to France ! Mumble, mumble, too much man. Nice trip up, especially the mountains. At the frontier I found I hadn't my passport, so I stayed at the border. The guards were great[8], then I climbed the mountain and picked a big bunch of flowers up there. It was really great, then sat on a memorial where 3 border guards had died in an avalanche. On the way up got 'Hendrix in the West' and 'Meddle' P.F. Met a Hawaiian girl coming through the border, her lift wasn't going far, so I said; if my amigos came (I'd been waiting for 6 hours) she could come. Got to Genoa, sat and talked to the girl driving (and played music) what was left of the morning. She was a Jesus freak just complete but not extreme, when Rob & Vic arrived I said, start praying for my passport and I found at some guys dropped in for a smoke twice. I crashed out and woke up, it was morning.

At 2 o'clock was sitting on the pavement reading Julie's letter when 2 cops put me in a car and took 3 of us to the station, where I was questioned, stripped to my pants and put in a room with more freaks. They must have rounded up everyone with long hair. I asked after 2 hours to see the consulate. They rapped on and for some reason no dice. Smiley[9] had called and had left a note.

---

[8] There is a passport stamp in my diary Moncenisio 28. 6 IU. 1972. This might have been that border crossing.

Got caught ripping off in a store[10]. Got let off, being a German.

SATURDAY – Smiley arrived, got 2 letters from mum saying come home. Started hitching to see Julie in Norway with Smiley. Arrived in Bellinzona at 11.30. Slept in some guys car. In the morning he bought us chocolate drink. Got a lift by a yank who bought us ham, bread and cake. Then a lift from the Swiss Doktor who bought us tea and cake. Then a lift from a soldier who took us round Zurich Airport, plus tea. Then to the border where we crashed at an Evangelical pad (Kreuzlingen).

Got to Allfalterbach practically in one lift. Stayed 3 nights, had lots of beer, watched TV, had typical food. Left Thursday at 2 o'clock, got to Strazburg, sent a couple of cards, then got a ride to 10 km near Paris. Stayed one day, slept near Belgium.

Went through on the 8th July, got a ride all the way to Amsterdam. Turned on 3 people who gave us a ride and slept in their tent. Next day put Smiley's gear at the airport. Split, met two people an English one, we're talking and a yank came over and said he was leaving the country and gave me a small pipe etc.
My impression of Amsterdam wasn't very good, maybe cause it rained solid and was so expensive.

MONDAY JULY 10th – Smiley left in the morning. Went to the park

---

[9] The Hawaiian girl.
[10] I don't remember this incident. They probably asked if I was German.

sent 4 cards, Julie, Jeanie, Pip, Vic and Rob. Got run over by a push bike but only bruised and torn trousers, saw a guy get busted in the square. Got to the frontier put a joint under the seat of a car I was in. They took my pipe and the car came back and the driver gave them the joint[11]. They searched everything then.[12] Then let me go, reached Duisburg next day, got rides to Baden Baden, bought a loaf of bread.

Got a ride to Karlsruhe then a lorry SWISS took me 200km to Basel, he bought me a coffee. Then at Basel it rained and I got a lift a third of the way to Luzern, then a motorbike picked me up to Luzern. Very nice guy, coffee long talk. Slept near Luzern, next day a ride to near Aldorf where I met 2 German American girls, got quick lifts with them, a guy bought me 2 liters of beer. Then the last lift we slept at his house.

FRIDAY – Next morning a ride to Milan, then a lorry to Genoa, more coffee. Slept in the van, saw Vic and Rob.

SATURDAY – Went to the hostel, got a letter from Julie, had a swim, slept in the van with the 2 German girls.

SUNDAY 15th July – At 4 o'clock in the morning, headed for Torino

---

[11] This incident has always cropped up when I have anything to do with the German authorities, concerning visas and so on. One joint 40 year ago!!!
[12] I remember in the end the cop said if I get caught again I get this: and he held his outstretched hand in front of his face and I said "five?" and he replied "no not five BARS".

where Rob and Vic have to work. Wrote to Julie.

Monday did very little, got stoned.

SATURDAY 29th July – For the last 15 days have done very little, got Neil Young single disc 'War Song'. Had my photo taken for a mag.[13] Took some photos in a booth, bought a brown Tye Die T-Shirt, wrote to Julie after a delay due to no envelopes. Also dropped Barry a line and a Maroc purse. Now I am hung up, anxiously every day I enquire for mail. I can't begin to wonder, I have an awful feeling something is very wrong. I must soon maybe Monday go to Mondane in France to send my rucksack home. Had the first feeling of real homesickness today and had to fight back the tears. For God's sake where's my letter from Julie?

SUNDAY July 30th – I am starting for Mondane today. No letter as the office was closed. Arrived at Mondane that night, slept by a river, bought Ron some Tabac. Next day climbed up a mountain and found a fort and garrison, the garrison dated 1938. I suspect the fort was Norman as it resembled Portchester so much. Found a hand pump dated 1890, it was a lovely day, don't know what to do about JC, wish she was here now, it's really beautiful. Today I'll treat myself to wine, no beer, chocolate, cigs, cake, French bread and cheese or something. I'll buy some film too. Had a big yogurt, beer, cheese and bread.

---

[13] Some guy approached me said he needed a picture of a Hippie for a magazine. I have never seen the picture though.

Slept half the night in a church the other half a Sunday school.
Wrote JC and mum, pack (rucksack) cost 27 francs.

Got a lift to Lanselbourg went to the hostel have got beer,
sausage and beans & bread for tea. Spent the day resting my feet
in icey stream water and taking photos, it's a really nice place, feel
like coming back sometime. With JC I expect.[14]

Next day had sausage & beans for breakfast, left about 12 o'clock.
Got a lift off 3 French students going to Istanbul. Soon as I hit
Rob's pad the 2 spade[15] chicks came out. I said "where was Rob"?
They replied "dunno". Went for 3 sandwiches a coke and milk.
Then got the letter from JC, I was shocked and hurt and didn't
have the guts to finish it. Had some soup, rice, yogurt and a
caramel. Kept poking at the letter. Left at 7 walked 4 hours in the
rain, felt like punishing myself. Got to the Autostrade entrance
had a sandwich and gave one to a couple of frogs, got a lift to
Tortona. Then a lift to outside Genoa, then a lift to walking
distance. Was approaching the town as the bells tolled 4 at 5. Was
in the main square, it was really strange and dead quiet. Started
for the hostel, had a coffee at 6 and at 6.30 the letter was in my
bag. Walked to the park about 1½ mile, bought bread and milk.
Had one sandwich then read the letter. Oh boy what a kick in the

---

[14] I did return some years later with my girlfriend from Berlin.
[15] This is not PC but at that time it was not meant as a derogatory term. It was
hip street language in those days.

balls. I felt wild and very destructive, smashed some glass and my yogurt cup. Then all of a sudden decided I had to suffer and would volunteer for Vietnam. Went to the Embassy at about 8 but no dice. I was so strong on the idea if they'd have had the forms, I would have joined. Started to hitch, no luck. Walked to Savona, read the letter again. "I'll never love you, I'll never love you" ringing in my ears. I put my face in my hands and unwillingly cried.

After that I got a great lift to Tortona on a motorbike. Then after some hours 20 miles outside Torino, then a truck into town. Found it hard to keep awake had some coffee and a doughnut, went to the train station where I am writing this. 4 fell asleep, 5.30, pigs[16] told me to go, sat in the park, wrote a letter to JC, took 5 hours. Slept in the station again, met a couple of West African dealers and later a Swede, had a smoke with him.

Next day nothing, slept mostly and then walked round all night. Next day bought coffee and 3 doughnuts, had a row with a cop. Have this urge to write to JC but I'll let her cool first. She's probably itching for an address so she can write a nasty. Tomorrow I buy some shoes as one of my feet's gone septic.

Next day bought some D. Boots and met a couple of yanks who taught me how to hassle money. Next day got some lire, met a GB chick who bought me a coffee and sandwich. Scored some acid

---

[16] A term used for cops in those days more descriptive than offensive.

and a smoke. Went for a swim in a local pool. Next day the yanks money came through and they bought a tent and a sack. I ripped a sleep bag. A guy well 2 gave me 9 mille apiece.

Went for a swim again. Bought an Indian vest.

Today is Thursday, I feel if nothing has happened.

LAST PAGE – *On the last page there are just some notes, part of a letter to Julie, the passport stamp, a shopping list and an address*:

Dear Julie, today we drove up to near the Swiss frontier, only on arrival I found I had left behind or lost my passport. So I.......

Algerciras _ Ceuta (Sebta)   Moncenisio 28. 6IU 1972

Tolul touole tal-you-are

MODANE : FILM CHOC FAGS (PLUM CAKE, TABAC, ALABAMA AND USED FILM IN RUCSACK)   GET A PASSPORT STAMP

FOOD CHEESE (Laughing Cow) Wine, Beans, maybe tinned fish.

Musile (Bircha)   MAZIO SANDRA, VIA ROMA N48, VENAUS 10050, (*TO*)

3. Road Trip with Barry wood (part two)

Written in an Italian notebook, says: NOME, MATERIA, SCUOLA "Orario Settimanale Delle Lezioni"[17]

FRIDAY 11th August – Bought a rucksack. Jack and Stewart split as their money had come. We said farewell and they laid on to a smoke. Met an English guy called Stephen. Slept by the river.

SATURDAY – Ate a lot, bought 3 bottles of wine and got given some smoke. Went round with 3 chicks, got pissed and crashed by the river.

SUNDAY – Split for Venice, met a soldier who bought me a beer. Got a ride to Milan then Venice. As I walked across the 4km long bridge, I thought how much the place was like Pompey. Met 2 GB guys who had come from Greece and crashed in the park.

MONDAY - Next day, got some beads and P. cards and food met 2 Germans caught a boat to the Lido island, had a fire, crashed on the beach.

TUESDAY – One of the Krauts[18] split. Sat around, reading and met

a GB couple on the beach. Crashed in the shade.

WEDNESDAY – The other Kraut split and in the afternoon the GB's did too. Had a swim lovely weather. Crashed by myself.

THURSDAY – Sat reading a book and scrounged fags and drank

---

[17] NAME, SUBJECT, SCHOOL "weekly timetable"
[18] Not PC and I can see I use the term German later. Kraut was not really a derogatory term in those days 'Kraut Rock' was descriptive. Originally an American term meaning German probably from Sauerkraut. UK term Jerry probably from Jerry Can was not used much.

tons of coffee. Slept OK in a tent with 3 Italians as it rained.

FRIDAY – had coffee the GB couple had met a couple of GB guys, had a chat. Then the weather which had been okay went into its second bad day, so 5 of us crashed in the cafe.

SATURDAY – Went to Venice by ferry bought a flick knife[19] and some sandals. Waited for the Thomas Cook Office to open, it didn't had hoped for a reply from Julie. Crashed in the shelter. I started eating spuds in their jackets.

SUNDAY – Rain again. I sent a postcard of VENEZIA [20] to Barry scribbled at the top it says in brackets (sent one week after arrival)[21] postmark 19th Aug.1972 To: Mr. Barry Wood, 12, Greenlands Road, CAMBERLEY, Surrey, England.

"Thanks for your letter. Got here yesterday. It was through bad luck my pack got ripped off and I lost the two chicks. And stayed in Torino 2 more weeks waiting for them. I am now so low on cash I had to spare change for a new pack, sleeping bag and harmonica. It's really hot and this place is crammed with Yank tourists etc. Figure I'll leave soon maybe hit Yugoslavia. Back on bread and cheese. But in Torino the spare changing was so good we had whole fried chicken and lots of good grub. Well look after yourself.

---

[19] For some reason I bought a switch blade, because you could not get them in the UK or for protection at the beach.

[20] This is a copy from the actual postcard.

[21] This means I started writing it the day after I arrived.

All the best to everyone. Keep off that Motorway ! Stephen"

MONDAY – Met two more GB guys 2 split for home.

TUESDAY – Went to Venice, got a letter from Julie and mum. One of the guys Larry split, spent the day with him before he left, bought JC a brooch.

WEDNESDAY – Woke up and Joe, Janet and Barry were gone, no goodbye, they didn't want to wake me I guess. I nearly started to cry as we had become pretty close. I liked them I guess.

THURSDAY – Then I met a lady with her daughter who was trying to tell me the name of a fish and said her niece would know and that's how I met Lucy. They were a Czech family but Lucy was now Dutch and the others were Austrian. That night we went to see what films were on. I found out 'Made' with Roy Harper was on and I was going to leave today as the pop concert with P. Floyd, E.L.P. , Donovan and The Stones was off. And Lucy was to be here a few days so I thought I'd stay, we had a drink and I walked her home.

FRIDAY – Saw her again, spent the day swimming, finding shells for the daughter then had a meal in the evening with them. After that we took a ferry and I cashed in £4 in Venice. Decided I may as well have a good time and I needed a new film anyhow. When we got home we sat outside a café on a swinging seat.

SATURDAY – Met again sunbathed took a few photos, had a pizza, had tea again with them and talked a long time with the lady, she said "you must always fight for what you want and never give up. Take all you have and build on it and try hard." I was very impressed. She said also to find the right girl you must go to the East, for there girls have good hearts and are not so corrupted by money search and you will find.

This evening I didn't take Lucy out cos she was drunk on wine so I took her straight home and went to my hut.

SUNDAY – We were together during the day and talked a lot, and I explained about JC and she talked about her boyfriend who she chucked, and had been out with others since but still thought of him. That evening I had tea with a nice English family; mussels, fish, pizza, wine, very nice people and the father was the head of something in some London University. He had spent one Christmas in Venice, with I think Germaine Greer, the head of Women's Lib. Anyway we had an interesting chat and I left to meet Lucy but I was late so I decided to get drunk. So I had 3 beers and walked off with the bottle and smashed it.

Then I found a Coke bottle and threw it down the road, then a bottle in a garage near a shop, then 4 more beers and 2 in a bar by the sea. Then Ice Cream, then I sat after a lot of fags on the seat we sat on before and I thought of JC and how glad I was I hadn't met Lucy and I started singing what I thought:

What'da you doing in Morocco ? When you wanna go home,
home.

Why are you heading for India. Is it just to be alone?

How are you sitting here ? It's a dam long way from home.

You think of her too often, And you don't quite know why.

Do you think all your roaming, Will teach you not to cry?

Do you think all your drinking, will help you at all?

And how many bottles is it now, you've smashed against the wall.

Don't you know life's a game? Our troubles they are all the same.

If you roam anymore, then my friend

Your just walking up to a locked door

What the fuck am I doing here? What is happening?

Then on the way home I just walked up to a guy sleeping on the park place and said "Hey man, mind if I talk to you? Do you speak English? I 'am kinda drunk, I guess you smoke?" he replied "You mean hash or what?" His name was Craig and he walked to the beach with me and crashed in the hut.
He wanted to be a lawyer, he was really interesting.

MONDAY – Went and said sorry I didn't show to Lucy and Co as they were leaving. As I waved the ferry goodbye I had to fight back the tears.[22] Not because of love for Lucy, there was none but

---

[22] I had just turned 18 in July this is close to the end of August. I had been alone on the road since mid March. I guess the emotional strain was starting to kick

they had all been real good to me. On the bus going back the tears rolled down my face and I felt a fool. Got back and talked to Craig, afterwards he split for Venice and I went and saw a couple of Charlie Chaplin films, trying to cheer up.

Then I managed to gate crash a Japanese movie, by luck, as the toilet was beyond the barrier. But it was a bloody bore to say the least. Craig saw it too, only he paid. We met back at the camp, had some wine. Then there was a terrific thunder and lightning storm. I just lied low and prayed we wouldn't get hit. It was really horrid, like being in a bunker getting shelled. I smoked 3 fags and had wine, even blew my harp to try and calm myself. In the morning I read this: *"Steve we still seem to be alive – cheers! I've decided to leave for Florence today. Will do some more things in Venice this morning and leave this afternoon. Thanks for everything. Have a great trip EAST. Craig"*

I felt sad I was now alone again. But the point is I've been meeting too many good people[23]. God I wish I wasn't. I hate goodbyes. Today I am going to try and gate crash Roy Harpers 'Made,' then tomorrow Wednesday I will split. Got into 'Made' okay took a bottle of Aqua Cadre bit like Vodka and a bottle of wine, drunk it in the cinema, lost my bag, met the producer John Mackenzie[24], spoke for a while. Then when I went outside, I fell down and spent the night in hospital.

THURSDAY – Tried to find my bag but some stupid cleaning lady had thrown it away. So when I thought I had caused enough

---

in.

[23] Kinda brings home the Dylan"many a road taken by many a friend, and each one I aint never seen again".

[24] He told me Roy was not there because he was very sick at that time. John took a long hearty pull on my bottle of wine. Like a man dying for a drink and trying to get to where I already was.

trouble, I split and bought a meal. On the beach I asked a guy for a fag and he got me a meal and 20 Rothmans and the next day he said he would like to talk to me again and he'd bring me a Russian coin. Got the coin and a meal then went on to Venice to take photos. Got a couple of letters from mum and one from Jeanie[25]?!! Who I aint heard from for a year. Had another meal and went back to the Lido.

(Here is an excerpt from the letter)[26]

"Dear Stephen, In the midst of my packing I realized I needed to write to you and tell you what is happening. Fred and I did not get married and are not going to ever – period - . It's so long and involved that I do not want to be bothered with it right now.

I have good maybe bad news for you. I'm coming to Europe in 3 or 4 weeks for a long, long time – a year or more. I'd like to meet you somewhere or maybe we could meet somewhere like you could pick me up from the airport when I arrive. Stephen it would be so sad if we didn't travel together but it looks sort of like it will be this way. I have no way of getting in touch with you. We just have to get in touch with one another.

I bought a two man tent and we could just go Helter Skelter. Oh Stephen - the places we could go together, the beauty we could see together! You sound like you are having some far out experiences. I'd like to go to Greece too and Yugoslavia. All the warm places when winter comes. Stephen, your age never meant a dammed thing to me. You are just a groovy person and I really loved you

---

[25] This was forwarded by my mum it was an Air Mail fold up letter, where you write on one side and the other side is the envelope. Post marked New York 15 Aug. 1972. Then to my home address in Camberley 19 Aug. It finally reached me in Venice Wagons Lits Cook Venezia 30 Aug 1972. In it she said I could reply until the 31st Aug when she would be splitting to Europe and we could meet up. I discovered later that she went to Jamaica instead.
This shows how spontaneously peoples plans could change.
[26] This was not in the diary but I have the letter.

for such a short time. This is really all I have to say but I will write again more specifically when I'm going to arrive etc. I've just been working, saving money. I'm working two jobs – nurse's aide and a cocktail waitress. Stephen if at <u>all</u> possible try to get in touch with me. I'll be at …..N.Y. Until August 31st. 1st week in Sept…..

P.S. I'm writing to your parents in case they may get in touch with you too.

Really hope to see you soon."[27]

SATURDAY – Roger bought me a jumper, had some food, washed my hair, got some tickets to see a movie by the French director Jean-Luc Godard

SUNDAY – Got the bus out of town to the Auto Strade, met an Italian, had some food, smoked and had a jam. Next day a lift in a GB truck to Rjiveck.[28] There had tea with an old man who didn't want to be forgotten and I won't forget him.[29]

NEXT DAY – A couple of rides and I got to Zagreb, all was cheap except the hostel. So I crashed out. Next day sent a letter to mum and JC and cards to Roberta and Barry. Ate like hell bought some brandy (slivovitz) and Tabac for Ron. May split today.

4th SEPTEMBER – Did split, saw Tito go through the town. Walked to the exit. Met a GB couple. All got a ride, stuck out in the middle of nowhere. Stayed in a motel 25 /- each. Next day 5th Sept. split up, got a lift by a guy to Kassel through Austria and Munich. He bought me some fish and spuds, travelled all night. He dropped

---

[27] I don't know what I replied. I can see from the diary that I was sending her postcards
[28] Yugoslavia.
[29] He had lived in the States and spoke good English, but on reflection he was a very sad case, living alone in the hills.

me off on the 6th Sept. at 7 o'clock in the morning. Got a ride by a bloke who told me of the murders at the Munich Olympics.[30] Then two yanks took me nearly to Hamburg. They dropped me off near a wood, it was like a dream, the moss was like a bed. Had coffee and crashed for 6 hours. Reached Hamburg, had food, scored in the train station. Some queer sailor bought me a meal, then I took off. Caught a mouse but it got away. Sent a card to the guy who gave me a ride to Kassel as I left my camera behind. Met an Israeli, spoke to him for a while, then crashed by the motorway.

I sent a postcard of ZAGREB to Barry dated 4th September 72[31]. To: Barry Wood, 12, Greenlands Road, CAMBERLEY, Surrey, England. (regards to all) The address you wanted : Noirot J......, Villa No. .., Les Bormetts, 83250, LA LONDE, France.

"Dear Barry, Looks like we should have come here first. They have these buffets all over the town where you can get beefburger and spud for 1/3 (old money) it's cheap as hell, big ice creams 2p just got a half bottle of brandy 4/- but besides that wish I wasn't here. I 'am now heading for Amsterdam to meet Julie on the 12th then probably home (groan). Been travelling alone mainly since I left Torino, stayed in Venice a month as that Roy Harper film was on. I took a bottle of wine and this cheap Vodka like stuff, sank them both and spent a comfortable night in hospital. Well that's all from behind the Iron Curtain. Stephen"

7th SEPTEMBER – Got a ride with 2 yank chicks to the Danish frontier. Then we were talking to 2 more yank chicks and all 5 of us got a ride in a van and all had a beer. Got a ride with the other two chicks to Kolding. Decided to stay there as they were heading

---

[30] He was an American who was married to a German and he was really pissed off at the British for letting Leila Khaled go.
[31] This is a copy from the actual postcard.

on to Copenhagen, decided not to push my luck. Found a neat camp and made coffee. Might stay here tomorrow as well.

8th SEPTEMBER – Changed £2, got some Levis, forks and spoon, food and a toy for Jill's kid. Then headed out, walked for a hell of a time and finally got a ride over the border[32]. There it was night and I asked a group of people for a fag, the family was GB, one Dane and a Mexican hitch hiker. Stayed in this families Rasthus[33], had chips and coffee. In the morning we drank beer till 3, then got a ride to the outside of Hamburg. A girl offered me a room but I wanted to reach JC. So I walked for 2 hours, asked a guy for help and he got me 3 beers and 20 Camels and a ticket on the underground, reached the Autobahn and crashed.

9th SEPTEMBER – Started walking down the road and got a ride to Hanover, then a lift about 100 keys then a ride to Hamm. So I thought I would look up a mate[34] but the driver read the address wrong and took me 20 keys out. Luckily I got a ride back but she was out. Then it rained like hell, walked 5km got soaked and it was great 2 people picked me up and took me to a friend's where I could stay.

11th SEPTEMBER – Changed £6 this day, bought a shirt some food and three liters of wine. Decided to take a train tomorrow. Had a terrific chicken dinner and in the evening we drank the 2 liters of wine, then went for beer. Got blind drunk then Reinhardt took me

---

[32] When I was leaving Denmark I walked through the border. My impression of Denmark was not good. I met a backpacker coming in and said to him "I've been all over Europe man and this country really sucks, you should turn around" he was a Dane returning home and apologized that I had not liked his country. The irony is I settled in Denmark in the late seventies and still live there!!!!

[33] I probably mean "Raststatte" which is a roadhouse or cafe.

[34] This was a girl I met in Camberley who was working on the Old Dean Estate as an Au-pair or exchange student

home. I threw up when he'd gone back to the pub.

12th SEPTEMBER – Woke up at a quarter to six and he said we had time till nine but I am so edgy about seeing JC, can't sleep. Reinhardt, 425 Bottrop, Osterfelderstasse. West Germany[35]. Caught the train ring, got it half price[36]. Got to the hotel to meet JC and was late, but walking near Dam Square I got a tap on the shoulder. Walked round talked then she split to her 17 guilder a night hotel and I stayed outside the station talking to a Norwegian guy called Ragnar.

13 SEPTEMBER – In the morning we sat in the café and dozed off for 10 minutes and when we woke his bag was gone. So we toured round then I met JC. Had a nice day, fell asleep on her lap in the park and she flipped out and paid for the sleep-in.

14th SEPTEMBER – Next day booked in at the Christian Hostel for 5 nights. Turned up at our meeting point late. So a couple of hours later I hopped on a bus towards her hotel and she got off the same bus crying and she was pleased to see me. Hate having to leave her at night. Slept great in the hostel.

15th SEPTEMBER – Breakfast 4 pancakes 2 coffees loads of bread and jam, price 2 guilders. Can't remember much of what happened, probably today we went to see 'Devils Brigade' pretty good movie. Afterwards saw a punch up in a bar.

16th SEPTEMBER – Remember very little of today it was probably wine and the usual quarrels but happy ending, maybe rain.

17th SEPTEMBER – Tomorrow she leaves so we or she went to Ann

---

[35] Name shortened.
[36] This was the only time I caught a train on my trip and only then because I had to meet JC in Amsterdam.

Frank's[37] house. I got a bottle of wine opened, we went to see a Western, then had our worst quarrel, was nearly the end. Then we went for a walk and coffee then she split.

18th SEPTEMBER – She took my bag. I done a mail check and wrote her a letter. Then I met a yank called Steve who reminded me of Reggie, he took me to a club and we toured the Red Light district. He used one.[38] Smoked about half an ounce then I gave a couple half a bottle of Slivovitz.

19th SEPTEMBER – We got back very late. I left the hotel, walked round town looking for a Neil Young single 'Dance, Dance, Dance' with 'Downtown' on the B side. Then got a ride to the bottom of Holland. Then great luck a German guy who I am sitting on the ferry with now is going to Liverpool. Thinking of phoning JC when I hit GB. But I don't know as this is the 1.30 ferry and it arrives early.

20th SEPTEMBER – And I am going to my homeland (BLISS) as JC would say. Got to London at 7.75 had a big meal in a café. Went to Hyde Park met an Aussie who'd been travelling two years[39]. Phoned JC had a meal at the Embassy, went to the Youth hostel, too much, so I slept in Holland Park after Fish & Chips.

21st SEPTEMBER – Phoned JC arranged to meet her in Guildford at 3 tomorrow. Went home all the same saw Simple.[40]

---

[37] I did not want to go in. I did not like the idea of looking in cupboards where people had hidden terrified.

[38] Not really my scene.

[39] We all had backpacks and an American guy with a backpack came over. He sat down blew out exhausted and said "Wow man, I'm really beat, I been on the road 10 weeks". Me and the Aussie exchanged looks. The guy inquired "How long you guys been travelling?" I said real deadpan about 7 months and the Aussie followed with "almost 2 years"!

[40] David Simpson. Old Dean Estate mate later worked in South Africa as a DJ..

22nd SEPTEMBER – Went to catch the bus met Scoanes[41] and Bland. Had my first Stout and Cider. Got the bus while waiting for the bus went to a bog in a store and met Mark and Pip[42], had a quick chat. Then caught the bus to Worthing. Booked for three nights in a B&B with JC. Had a Chinese meal.

23rd SEPTEMBER – Went for a walk bought a book, went in pubs, had a meal

24th SEPTEMBER – Sunday, saw a movie. Not much doing got back early.

25th SEPTEMBER – Bought an LP, got the bus JC caught a train home. Got home met Paddy[43] on the way.

4. Jeanie from the U.S.A.

That was the end of the diary as a written record. I have not changed anything. The only things I have added are some footnotes and Jeanie's letter from Venice. Reading it now 40 years later many of the incidents I don't remember. Many of the people

---

[41] Stephen Soanes. Old Dean Estate mate.

[42] This was quite a funny incident. I had not seen Pip for a long time and just stood next to him in the John and said "how you doing Pip?" and we burst out laughing.

[43] Paddy from Frimley. .

I met I do remember, and in some places I have added a description of them in the footnotes. I do not remember keeping this diary on the journey or even how come I still have it. I found it in a suitcase amongst some letters. I kept some letters from people like Jeanie who were important to me at that time in my life. Now by coincidence her letters become appropriate and fit into the script like pieces of a puzzle. I did try to search for Jeanie on the net but had no luck. (*Perhaps she is dead, moved or married*). It would have been good to compare notes. It would be interesting now after 40 years have passed, to see if any dreams got fulfilled. I met her at that fateful Grand Funk Railroad concert in Hyde Park on July 3rd 1971. Setlist: 1, Are You Ready 2, Paranoid 3, In Need 4, Mark Says Alright, 5, T.N.U.C. 6, Inside Looking Out (The Animals cover) 7,Gimme Shelter (The Rolling Stones Cover). She sent me a card 21 days later when I turned 17, we then corresponded for about two years but never met again. I had forgotten all this with the passing of time. I had not forgotten her but I had forgotten the sequence of events. We wrote for a long time but I was not aware we kept in touch so long or during this period. Her letters had a very profound effect on me and really encouraged me to do my own thing. In that way she was very American. She seemed to see through all the bullshit that working class kids in England had been conditioned to accept, through their upbringing. She wrote to me a year later in 1973. I never received the letter; I found it when I was clearing my mum´s house in 1993. It brought back memories and made some things clearer. She had just been reading through all my old letters and wondered how I was doing. Here is an excerpt that reflects on the time. From her words I got the sense that she had finally found some peace in her life:

"My life is slowing down Stephen. I'm changing rapidly and not so strung out with loose end desires. Reading back over the letters you've written to me, I see in them my changing. When I reread your letters it was like meeting you all over again. What a difference – like reading them again for the first time. You were growing then also – confused, bewildered – envious – hateful – love, love, love – happy, happy love. Free as a mountain wind. How have you changed Stephen? Are you taller? Have your shoulders gotten broader and stronger. Where is your innocence? Where are you in terms of the universe? Stephen, are you in love X. (All your letters have staggered kisses throughout them)

Last September I fully intended to come travelling with you to Europe and then I went to Jamaica. You see I was blinded then by jealous, possessive love and was bound up and dueling in darkness. Now my mind is cracked with light and freedom is in the making"….. "So sad. It's been such a long time since we've written that you might be dead, married or moved."

In a way, when I read this so many years after she had wrote it, I felt a sense of relief that she never came to Europe. She went to Jamaica that meant we had not missed each other, she had gone somewhere else. In the letter she goes on to say, that she wanted to visit Britain again in August, and suggests that maybe we could tour the country together. So she had not lost the travelling itch! The sentence she wrote towards the end of the letter is illuminating. I guess those were the three options a guy had back then; 'dead, married or moved'. When I read that today and think about what might have happened if we had met again.

Sometimes people's lives pass like ships in the night. Close enough to see each other but moving in different directions. I have included these excerpts of her letters because like I said her letters meant a lot to me in my formative years. Jeanie had beautiful prose and a wonderful way with words that are expressive and representative of the times. I really hope life has been good to her along the way.

5. Reflections

I look upon this diary as a historical document. I have no wish to account for or defend anything that happened in it. I can only confirm that it did happen. To understand the past you cannot judge it by the values we have today. I have not adjusted things to make them acceptable in today's world. Some of the things written might put me in a negative light. A lot of people were kicking against the system back then. Many of them were pretty messed up. I was probably a bit of both, perhaps more of one than the other! I surprised myself by some of the terms I used back then but I have left them in. Much of it was street language that did not have the negative connotations back then that it has now. Another aspect of that journey when I think about it, is how strange life is sometimes. How the people you meet and the decisions you make contribute in some ways to defining your destiny. How memories of some people whose paths you cross during life's journey stay with you for the rest of your life and some fade. Thanks to the internet I have recently made contact again with Pip, Barry and Paddy after a 30 year break. I have tried to analyze a bit what and why things happened back then without much success. I think wanting something different from what our parents had was a major driving force. Jeanie's other letter that I mention later, illustrates how for the Young Americans it was a very political thing, whereas for me and Barry I think it was much more of a class thing. We were both stuck in the working class rut of what was then a class ridden British society and wanted something different. Did we achieve anything in the end? I think I can say we broke the chain as far as our kids are concerned. Barry's three daughters and my two sons have better educations and better prospects than we had back then. Our world view was definitely broadened, especially when it comes to what you can do and not do with your life. For my part I never lived in England again on a permanent basis. I enjoyed visiting over the years but no longer feel a strong connection. I don't know Barry's entire story; maybe one day he will write it himself. He was always into meditation and has continued to follow that path through his life on various levels. He took a camera on our trip and was always interested in the visual side of things. He still takes very nice nature photographs of the English countryside and does metal detecting (still searching for something). In much the same way I continued studying as I got older (still looking for clues). Here are some of the things he wrote to me when I asked him if he could remember anything that inspired him to go on the road and any memories of what happened when he came back. I had lost Barry round about the 8th of June 1972 on our trip. He met two Dutch guys in Menton and headed north. They stayed in a deserted Hostel for a while in the Swiss Alps. Spending their time drinking at the local pub and hanging out. They found stuff like cow bells on the mountain and sold them to tourists. He travelled to Amsterdam with them and as he explains in his mail got a job there and came home in September. I can see from my diary I sent cards to him and the odd souvenir. I have fondest memories of lying on his bedroom floor very stoned, listening to all four sides of 'Tommy' by 'The Who'[44];

They were singing something about going on an amazing journey and riding together. The lyrics were beckoning you to go on that adventure, to open the door at the back of the wardrobe or walk through the mirror.

6. Barry's Story

(First mail) "Hi Steve, the camera I used was a German make can't remember what but as u said it was a good one later sold it on eBay for a few quid, shame.

I was always interested in going somewhere as a kid, even as a toddler I run away. To the circus was found 4 years old up Park Avenue. I remember watching a TV travel show about an old guy who tramped it around Europe before the war. Wanted to do the same and of course there was the whole Hippy thing: hit the road, drop out. And working in the factory was like death for a 18 year old, like you said we were working with people who had to fight a war bless em, but they seem to want the same for us. All I needed was someone who had the courage to want to do the same and with a little cash and a bit naive we set into the unknown what an adventure, we didn't have a return ticket lol.

(Second mail)   Left job in Wokingham they were going to put

---

44 Tommy the first Rock Opera. 1969 ©The Who

me on nights big motivation for leaving. Left school summer of 1969, no job school never talked about what u were going to do, went to Youth Labour Exchange , bloke pulled out a file with loads of vacancies no unemployment then thanks to Harold Wilson, said this is what you're going to do, sent me to builders merchants counter, manager didn't like my long hair got the sack 2 months later, dad got me a job in a dark room as that was my interest with a PCB company in Blackwater made redundant next year got the job in Wokingham etc. Couldn't wait to hit the road, found like minded friend who wished to go to lol.

Life I believed was going nowhere for me just the prospect of work no career prospects at all. Was extremely interested in the counter culture movement that came out of the sixties my ideal was to have some land or live in a commune with my chick lol.

A rebel without a cause or a job. I was interested in screen printing it was a skill and could be artistic (ANDY WARHOL). Did do some art prints at the time still got some.

'Main Street' was the album at the time.

Got back September, my brother remembers me walking down our road he said I had a long staff and looked like Jesus, and smelt like hell. Mum cooked me a big meal couldn't eat it, it was too much, my stomach had shrunk.

Yes left from Amsterdam was living in Vondal Park with the hippy scene, they now called where we camped hippy something it's an historical place to visit now lol.

Worked in a gherkin factory for a bit became chief inspector of gherkins, bastards never paid me. Also had a room at the University of Amsterdam painted it with Hindu symbols and got chucked out thought they would like it. Just had enough money for ferry to Harwich. Thumbed it to London picked up by a queer who thought I would go back to his flat had to leg it when he went for a pee. Got to Waterloo they were playing Lennon's universe song: "nothings gonna change my world".

Still makes the hairs stand on the back of my neck when I hear it. Will think of more about the trip for tomorrow hope this helps bas.

(Third mail)

Hi Steve, me and Paddy flew out to Morocco with a one way ticket, Paddy got robbed in the Kasbah the first day, also had his passport nicked on a beach. Got mugged in FEZ decided to leave, ate all our dope couldn't get off the bed, missed the ferry out,

Paddy must be the only person to smuggle acid into Morocco and Spain. We met a big German in Almeria Paddy showed him the acid he grabbed it out of his hand and took all ten tabs, we left in a hurry, always wondered what happened to him hope he's come down by now. Barry"

(Fourth mail) OK Steve, have a few more photos ps after 72 I also went to Greece just remembered only there for 3 weeks came

home left a bus load of nurses on there hols, lol Fool.

(Barry talked about some of the things that inspired him and mentioned Laurie Lee. A British poet who went on the road when he was 19 in 1933. He carried a tent, a violin, box of treacle biscuits on a journey to London that took him a month. He worked as a builder and then travelled to Spain living rough and busking with the violin. As he was very young he absorbed the atmosphere and describes it in his book:

'As I walked Out One Midsummer Morning'[45]

Barry mentioned to me that he went to Amsterdam with Paddy on the way back from Morocco. Later he went to Amsterdam with Pip but only for a holiday as he came back after three weeks. Someone was stabbed in the 'Sleep In'[46] there and he remembers it as having become quite a heavy scene. He thinks he must have had a job lined up that's why he went back so soon. Pip must have carried on for a while.

7. Pip and Paddy

Of the group of friends Pip travelled extensively, he was the first to leave Camberley when he went to London. He stayed in London for three months then he returned to Camberley and later travelled to Amsterdam with Barry.

---

[45] Laurie Lee "As I walked out one midsummer morning" Andre Deutsch 1969
[46] Type of hostel in Holland.

Pip remembers the car Nick Tesco drove up to Liverpool and the story about the carbon monoxide poisoning. He recalls that the car was bought from a neighbour in his street by a guy called Howard.

Pip worked for a while on the motorway together with Paddy, building the M3. The wages there were pretty good for the time; £25 a week. After Barry went back to England Pip left Amsterdam and hitched to Yugoslavia with an Irish guy and then took the train to Greece. He spent a few months on the island of Ios, and then took the boat to Egypt. The war broke out with Israel. He got arrested and let go, then got dysentery. He remembers wiring home to his folks saying "there's a war on please send money". They sent him about £40 which was a considerable amount at the time and enough to get the boat back to Greece and from there get the bus back to the UK. Once home he was diagnosed with hepatitis from the dirty water in Egypt. He says *"I got the taste then although it was never as exciting again (probably just as well)"*. Pip finally settled in Leeds.

Pip says he sees a difference in the way the group of friends split up in that I just left and never came back and the others slowly went off in different directions. Barry got married and had kids and did his thing and there was not the kind of close network remaining as I had imagined.

I see Pip in many ways as being an originator in our group. He had the advantage of coming from a middle class background where you are raised to think and question things. In my working class childhood you were brought up to know your place (which in Barry's and my case, was on the factory floor). He went to grammar school which gave him a good education. He rebelled very early against his parents and had to sleep rough for a while, whereas me and Barry left home and went on the road. We could return without problems as long as we paid rent. Generally we were left alone and could do as we pleased. On the other hand, Pip's parents read the Times,[47] and were wise to what young people were doing as far as drugs went. They followed what was happening in society. I would guess he had to leave home because he felt he was being controlled. (I do remember his mum looking into his eyes to see if his pupils were dilated). Most working class parents lived in ignorant bliss of what was happening in the world. Especially where drugs were concerned, they could never fathom what was going on. I have Pip to thank for turning me on to Neil Young and introducing me to a very different set of people, who were leaning towards the counter culture. They were very different to the Smoothie set that I was hanging out with at 'Reading Top Rank'.

I have not said much about Paddy. This is not because there is not

---

[47] English newspaper.

much to tell, but because Paddy was a true child of the sixties and does not remember anything.

(As the expression goes *"if you can remember the sixties you weren't there."* Well Paddy was most definitely there).

He was by nature a very caring person and a real laugh to be with. He was an axis our group evolved around and I believe we all owe him something in many ways. He was a good mate and we looked out for each other.

There is a lot to be said for young people to be exposed to many different ways of living while they are young. It really helps them find out what lifestyle suits them. I cannot overemphasize the importance of being accepted in a group where you feel you can be yourself. We were a close knit group of friends in Camberley in those days where people knew each other. The different crowds hung out at different pubs with names like 'The Wheat Sheaf' or 'The One Oak' and 'The Jolly Farmer' (although I don't recall ever going to the last one). I guess looking back it was not all bad. I have written an 'Outro' containing what I remember about the different things that happened after I came back.
It ends with me in Canada in 1975.

8. Outro – (postscript)

What happened after that is pretty vague in my memory. I

remember things but not in the correct sequence. The passing of time has erased things from my memory and my selective memory has left out events that I either wanted to forget or did not make a lasting impression on me. Memory and time are strange partners. Time while contributing to the other by creating new memories as it passes, erases some of what has gone. This is one of the reason history is so interesting. Why did people write something at a certain time or keep records during certain events. I had a friend whose dad had kept a diary or notebook during the Second World War. He had gone through D-Day and the invasion of Germany. She found the notebook after her father had died. Keeping a diary was something he had never done before or after. He had never talked about it or shown it to anyone while he was alive. My friend feels he kept a record for his family in case he did not return.

It is fortunate for me that I kept a diary of our trip because it documents the journey. I do not remember the original motivation for writing it and in fact had completely forgotten it in a box of letters in a suitcase for over 35 years. I do not remember how I managed to hang on to it as I travelled round quite a lot before I settled down and got married. With married life came responsibility, stability and routine and when kids are growing up work takes priority. I am very happy that I kept it as it is quite common to think when you are young *"I will remember this moment forever"* when you experience something you want to remember. Or you are lying on a beach in Greece, gazing at the stars with the music from a distance beach bar floating through the air around you, someone singing about: Feeling good being easy and Bobby singing the blues…. You think *"I want to cherish this moment and always remember it"*. Sometimes you do, sometimes you don't. But you rarely remember the smaller details about what you ate or who you met or where you moved onto when you left the beach. In reality the memory fades and you make general assessments for periods in your life "it was the happiest time of my life". It is unfortunate that most people who made those journeys back then did not keep records of their experiences. Books of course were written by writers and journalist but you did not get the personal documentation like you had from other periods in history. Bill Byson took the classic American backpackers trip to Europe the same time as me in 1972 only he went alone but he went back again in 1973 with his friend Stephen Katz. Twenty years later he tried to retrace some of his steps in his book 'Neither Here Nor There'. He intertwines his modern experience with recollections from the first two trips making some vivid descriptions that I am sure most Americans who made that journey would recognize. He mentions that the only cheap flights to Europe in those days were in old planes from New York to Luxemburg, with a refueling stop in Reykjavik. He describes the passengers as all being hippies except for a couple of business people travelling first class. He compares it more to a Greyhound bus going to a folk singers convention with musical instruments and wine. You get the impression that it just stops short of having chickens flying around the plane.[48] However it is a very short recollection that lasts only a few pages. On that trip in 1972, Bryson wandered round Europe, (UK, Ireland, Scandinavia, Germany and Italy) for four months. He recalls it as one of the happiest summers he had ever had. I think most people who went on the road back then would agree that the American experience varied from the European one in that they could afford to stay in hotels while many Brits slept rough or stayed in hostels. I do not mean that in a derogatory way, it was just my impression that their dollars went further and things were cheaper for them in Europe compared to the States. But no doubt, they paid their dues just like we did and in my experience Americans were always good company on the road (and still are). Barry and I met one in Hyde Park after the Grand Funk concert. He had long hair and an orange framed backpack[49].

"Man I just worked some clown job all winter to save up for this trip. You guys see the film Woodstock? That's how the world should be man, millions of people and everyone just grooving"

---

[48] ©Bill Bryson. Neither Here Nor There, (travels in Europe) Black Swan 1991,
[49] Americans were identifiable by these bright coloured framed backpacks that were expensive and not so common in Europe.

Barry was very amused at his description of factory work (which was what we did) as 'a *clown job*.' Many Americans stayed at hostels as well. In some ways they had a very different attitude that is quite hard for me to define. I think that I wanted a different kind of life on a personal level whereas for many Americans the focus seemed to be on changing their society on a collective level. The changes in European society and American society did eventually come about through what happened in the sixties and early seventies and I am sure many Americans experienced similar changes to mine in their personal lives. Half a year before Barry and I made our sojourn to Europe, I got a letter from my friend Jeanie[50] in the States dated November 9th 1971.

I give an extract in length as it clearly illustrates the feeling of the time. The anti - American sentiment and her remarks about the flag might make it difficult reading today and parental guidance is recommended. The world has changed a lot since then but unfortunately America is still at war as it was back then. Therefore I don't condone any of the sentiments in this extract of the letter. However I strongly feel that her statements are very relevant to our understanding of that period. Her answer shows how much more politically aware many Americans were in comparison to their UK counterparts.

"Your letter showed me the great difference between your youth

---

[50] The same girl I got the letter from in Venice during my road trip.

in Britain and our youth in the US. I have felt this before sitting in a pub in England that I will tell you about later. Past generations here in America have, through bloodshed (so bloody) and misery, made our generation able to do things that we dam well please for the most part – we have booming technology and abundant wealth and so much other <u>SHIT</u> that we are literally drowning in it. England's industries were checked making her economy an even balance. One generation after the other will basically be the same. No big worries other than saving money and earning a living for maybe a family later on. For the most part, this is how it is on the younger scene in England. In your big cities kids go to discotheques, look for new duds to wear. What is happening with a growing number of kids in America – that is what I would wish would happen in England. We (I use that collectively) have turned in horror and disgust and great disillusionment, from the outside world and turned our eyes inward to find out how to make ourselves cope with the disease that we see all around us. John Lennon sings about the world he sees in his song "Imagine". George Harrison's album "All Things Must Pass" is my all time favourite. Your guy Neil Young sings about the world's blindness to its aggression and its terrible end in "After the Goldrush". I guess what I am trying to say is that kids here have turned around and looked at their parents own bloodshed and saw what they gained – all futile efforts- the (parents) just gave: pride, religion, country,

that draw lines and limits on human beings. It tells them who to
believe in (the flag – piece of shit it is) the above three divide
people, bring hate and death. I want life and love. "Imagine all the
people, living life in Peace". That's my dream. It is so difficult for
me to write this as I know you could understand me so much
better if I could be there talking to you the way I feel right now. I
seek the "humanness" in people. In everyone it lurks there to be
bought out."

I was 17 years old when I read that letter and it gave me another
view of the world. I was a factory boy living on a council estate,
two up two down. Friends like Jeanie showed me there was
another world out there but it doesn't come easy. Five months
later Barry and I were packing our rucksacks to head out there.
I don't remember the departure from my family. No one offered
to drive me and Barry's dad Sid drove us both down to
Southampton. Barry said one of his dad's workmates had told his
dad "the trip will make a man of him." So I think his departure had
been more amicable than mine. People wished him all the best.
Old guys at his factory patted him on the back and wished him
luck. A lot of our fellow workers back then had seen service
abroad during WW2. One old guy I worked with had even been in
the trenches in WW1!! Now together, we stood at machines all
day long scrapping the chaff away from the cutting bit on the
lathe, waiting for the tea break. It wasn't quite like the workers in

Fritz Lang's 1927 film 'Metropolis'. But when you think about it, not much had really changed. You clocked in at 8 o'clock and clocked out at 4 o'clock. You waited for payday and Friday night, followed by the weekend, your two days of freedom.

That was the inspiration for me to put this together as a historical document and not as a personal statement. I would not condone the things that happened then but one should remember they happened to a whole generation. It started as a counter culture and somehow became integrated with mainstream life. Many of the things today evolved from young people wanting something different back then. Like Country Joe said to an interviewer who was wearing a bright coloured shirt, something along the lines of that he "could not wear a bright shirt like that if the sixties had not happened."[51] People tend to forget just how conservative and straight men dressed back then, people serving in shops always wore suits. Many of the personal freedoms we have today and the self determination about how we live our lives owes a lot to the sixties and early seventies. Many people's lives changed because of what they did back then and what they were influenced by. I think in my case my life took a very different direction than it would have if I had stayed in the factory. Here is a short summary of events as I remember them after I got back from the road trip I had started with Barry:

---

[51] Film Woodstock diaries.

I got a job at the Frimley Park Military Establishment where I worked as a gardener. I probably saved some money. The following year I went to the Island of Sark in the Channel Islands with JC. Our relationship ended there when she met somebody else and we split up. I moved on to Guernsey and worked in a café for a couple of months. I saved up for a gold ring with leaf decorations on it. I hung out a lot at the local Folk Club where they played folk music and had guests like Jasper Carrot. Then out of the blue Paddy wrote to me that I should come back to England because he had bought me a ticket for the Stones concert at Wembley, Empire Pool, London. The Stones played on the 7th – 9th September 1973. This is one of the set lists[52] : Brown Sugar / Gimme Shelter / Happy / Tumbling Dice / Star Star / Angie / You Can't Always Get What You Want / Dancing with Mr. D / Heartbreaker / Midnight Rambler / Honky Tonk Women / All Down the Line / Rip This Joint / Jumpin' Jack Flash / Street Fighting Man.

Paddy, Barry and me were heavily into The Stones and these were some of our favourite tracks. I do not remember the concert that well. Barry went on one of the other days with a guy called Ronald Maxted, he might have come with us as well on the second day. Paddy seems to think Barry was with us:

---

[52] I got this information from "setlist.fm" by Googling the Stones Goats Head Soup Wembley there were different sets. Not sure if this was the actual one. They vary a bit.

"Goats head soup wasn't it …..twas 3 of us ,,u brought some duty free whiskey from Guernsey... I was pissed before it started…..ended up on a park bench with a migraine after....didn't have any smoke drank whiskey instead ..big mistake"

I remember Barry said the day he went the security were working people over and Jagger stopped the concert and said "Aye mate this is our concert, leave them alone" and the security were jeering him but they backed off when Keith Richards went forward. (People knew better than to mess with old Keef) I remember being high up on the left hand side and Jagger running up and down the stage waving at people. Respect where it is due, Jagger might have dressed very effeminate but not many entertainers could have handled the situation like Jagger did at Altamont in 1969 telling the Angels to be cool.

On my return to London I squatted in an empty house in Kennington close to the tube station with an Irish guy called Frank who I had met on Guernsey. Lots of things happened at the squat and the scene soon turned quite heavy. I got beaten up by some heavy Scottish dudes who stole my radio, budgie and watch. Their leader was called Scotch Bob and he and his band of thugs generally terrorized the peaceful people who were squatting. They were always threatening girls and so on, really nasty pieces of work. I put a big sign up in the street saying "Desolation Row". They did not like that, when they jumped me in the street I actually saw stars when they knocked me out. Frank eventually found us a job in construction through some Irish contacts. While we were squatting we met a Swiss guy called Urs who stayed with us. With Frank I was working a lot but not saving any money because we were always in the pub. One payday we decided to hitchhike to Switzerland and visit Urs. It must have been winter when we left, because on the 5th of November 1973 I managed to see Neil Young with the Santa Monica Flyers at the Rainbow Theater in London. (The support band was the Eagles playing lots of material from their new LP Desperado.) Ticket price in the stalls was £2.50!!!! The Santa Monica Flyers were Neil Young – vocals, guitar, piano, harmonica, Ben Keith - pedal steel guitar, piano, vocals. Nils Lofgren - guitar, piano, accordion, vocals. Billy Talbot - bass, vocals. Ralph Molina - drums, vocals. Setlist:[53]

Tonight's the Night / Mellow my mind / World on a String / Speakin' Out / Albuquerque / New Mama / Roll Another Number / Tired Eyes / Tonight's The Night / Flying on the Ground is Wrong / Human Highway / Helpless / Don't Be Denied / Cowgirl in the Sand.

The show lasted two hours and the material was quite unknown. I had never heard "Tonight's the Night" at that time. I think he got bad reviews from the music papers but I enjoyed the show. Neil wore shades and a stripped jacket starting the show with

---

[53] Information from Sugar Mountain Neil Young Setlists.
http://www.sugarmtn.org/show.php?show=197311050

"Welcome to Miami Beach Ladies and Gentlemen" there were Palm Trees and a Wooden Indian. I recognized "Helpless" from CSN& Y and "Cowgirl in the Sand" from his LP "Everybody Knows this is Nowhere" and "Flying on the Ground is Wrong" from his Buffalo Springfield days. I was pretty loaded even before the show started and when the Eagles came onstage and introduced themselves "We're the Eagles from LA" and broke into "Take it Easy" the place lifted 6 inches off the ground and just blew me away. Neil Young said later in an interview that if Buffalo Springfield had stayed together they probably would have sounded something like the Eagles. It was a great concert. Afterwards outside at the stage entrance Bernie Leadon was standing with a group of guys next to a Mini Cooper. He showing them some riffs on a Fender Stratocaster plugged into a small pig nose amp that he had put on the roof of the car. I walked over to him and congratulated him on a really great show, he nodded, a really cool guy. Then Neil Young came by with his head down and a 'coat hanger' of people around him escorting him to his bus or car. You could see the difference: The Eagles were basically unknown in London back then and could walk round pretty free. But Neil Young was probably pretty tired of being hassled by fans all the time. A bootleg exists of this gig and although the sound quality is not that good it still catches the feeling of the time. Another concert I saw, this time together with Frank was Roy

Harper at the Royal Albert Hall on the 2nd of December 1973. Roy did material from his LP "Lifemask", Frank had never heard of Roy Harper and said afterwards that he really loved the concert. I had seen Roy quite a few times over the years. Back in Camberley Barry, Pip, Paddy and I were all pretty dedicated fans who followed his career. So Frank and I must have split for Europe soon after that. I don't remember exactly when we left England but must have been around then. I remember on the way down to Bern where Urs lived we spent Christmas in a Youth Hostel maybe in Switzerland or Germany. We celebrated with an American guy who reminded me of Bill Bryson (a lot of Americans on the road had that look, shaggy hair and full beard) he gave me a roach clip for Xmas. I had never seen one before. Unlike our American cousin's people in the UK generally did not use them. I guess because if you got busted by the cops it is pretty obvious what it was for. He used expressions like *'Mind Games'* that I was not familiar with. The American was a nice guy and we got high a few times. We had dinner together with him and his mate who was very straight and working as a tennis coach. I have fond memories of getting back to the hostel pretty drunk and talking intensely into *'the big white phone'*[54].

Later on the journey we celebrated a really great New Year's Eve at the Youth Hostel in Freiburg. Everyone snuck out after the

---

[54] The loo

curfew and lit a camp fire in the woods. We were all just young people having fun. I remember at least one guy who was an American serviceman stationed in the Air Force in Germany. After Switzerland Frank and I ran out of money and split up. I was really at a down point broke and did not know what to do. Frank went to his Embassy and got a ticket back to Ireland. I met an American in the Youth Hostel in Frankfurt who was just coming back from Israel. He gave me a really neat watch strap with a dust cover; he had a whole batch he was taking back to the States. He said I should try and get to the States and as I did not have the money for the fare he suggested I join the US Army. "There's a war on man, they take anyone". Now of course with hindsight I cannot believe I would contemplate such a thing. But back then I was basically homeless and broke and a lot of yank servicemen were as turned on as anyone else, if not more. We went to the American base at Frankfurt and I tried to join up. But the sergeant that interviewed me said they did not recruit people in Europe. He told me if I went to the States I could just go into any recruiting office and they would take me. It is notable that he made no comment on my long hair. I am pretty sure if it had been the English military they would have been much more judgmental. The Americans had the draft at that time and I am sure the sergeant had seen recruits from all walks of life. In retrospect I am of course glad none of this happened. But I still had a problem and did not know what to do, so I went to the British Council and tried to join the RAF from there. This sounds crazy now but I had applied once before. But I went to work in the factory instead. The British Armed Forces have always been a refuge for young working class men. At the British Council they told me that it was possible to enlist in Kaiserslautern. I remember trying to get a lift for hours in the rain. I finally got a lift in a Citroen 2 CV with a girl who had her daughter with her. She was going to Berlin and when the road split towards Kaiserslautern I looked out at the rain and decided to continue to Berlin.

9. BERLIN

The girl who gave me the lift to Berlin knew a student collective where I could stay in and dropped me there. I had a guitar with me and hung out with the Folk music crowd there. I made friends with a German guy called Christian who was the guitarist in the band Morgenrot and hung out with them a lot. I even wrote some songs for them that they never used. I remember the bassist Lutz had an LP I was really interested in by Bruce Palmer from the Buffalo Springfield. It was released in 1971 called *"The Circle is Complete"*. Then one day I fell in love with a girl I met while we were watching an American busker outside the Berlin Technical University which is on the Straße des 17. Juni.[55] Her name was

Anni and she really had a profound influence on my life. We hung out for a while. Then I teamed up with another English Folk guitarist and a French guy who played the Flute. We were all at a party and the French guy turned up with a fellow countryman who had a car and wanted to go to Paris but did not have money for petrol (a similar situation to the one with Nick Tesco going to Liverpool) I had been working and had a few Deutschmarks so off we went. When we got to Paris the guy parked the car in a side street and split. The flute player knew a guy where we could crash at his pad. I think I played "House of the Rising Sun" at one end of the Metro and the other guy played "You've Got to Hide Your Love Away" at the other end. We played until we had enough to buy a bottle of red wine and some bread and cheese, then relaxed. I was arrested once by the Police when I was busking or just sitting on the street and they threw me in a room full of French CRS riot police. Really heavy looking guys with facial scars but fortunately they left me alone. The pig who interviewed me was pretty miffed because I was clean (i.e. not carry drugs) and he had to let me go. I guess we busked for about two weeks. I remember another incident where the French guy and I were sitting on the Metro platform playing for fun. The acoustics were great the flow of a Spanish guitar nylon strings accompanying a flute sounded really good. Then a Metro employee came down

---

[55] 'Street of the 17th June'

and said he was very sorry it sounded really nice but we had to stop. When we stopped and all the people on the other platform were smiling and applauded. The two sides of French officialdom the cop and the Metro guy. Then the French guy split for Bordeaux where he lived and I returned with the other guy to Berlin.

On my return to Berlin in February or March 1974 Anni and I became a couple. I got a job as a civilian labourer at RAF Gatow and she started to study and taking on part time work. We travelled as much as we could and loved being on the move. For twenty days from the 2nd of April to the 22nd in 1974 we visited Nordfriesland, the island of Amrum in Northern Germany. We stayed in hostels and met some really nice people. One young German guy I remember lost the ability to play the blues because he was out of the city. I really laughed with him and said "it's all the sunny beaches man. You need a dirty city to play the blues". In the summer of 1974 we went grape picking in France and got into a Grateful Dead concert in Dijon on September 18th. Setlist:[56]
First set :
Uncle John's Band / Jack Straw / Black-Throated Wind (Bob Weir song) / Scarlet Begonias / Mexicali Blues / (Bob Weir song) Row Jimmy / Beat It on Down the Line (Jesse Fuller cover)

---

[56] http://www.setlist.fm/setlist/grateful-dead/1974/unknown-venue-dijon-france-1bd6055c.html

Deal (Jerry Garcia song) / The Race Is On (George Jones cover)

To Lay Me Down (Jerry Garcia song) / Playing in the Band

(Bob Weir song)

Second set:

Loose Lucy / Big River / (Johnny Cash cover) Peggy-O Play / (John

Strachan cover) Me and My Uncle (Judy Collins cover) Eyes of the

World / China Doll / He's Gone / Truckin / Drums / Caution (Do

Not Stop on Tracks) / Ship of Fools / Johnny B. Goode

(Chuck Berry cover) Encore: U.S. Blues.

It was a great show. Afterwards we went into their tour bus and

spoke to them for a while. We asked for a ride but they were

going another way (Bob Weir shouted; "nice try man").

After the grape picking we hitched through Spain to Morocco. I

remember getting vaccination shots at the border before we took

the ferry. I was trying to communicate with the nurse in my non-

existent Spanish and she just threw the needle into my arm and

gave me the shot. Everyone talked about not getting busted in

Franco's Spain because they locked you up and threw away the

key. No lawyer could get you off. We stayed the first night in

Ceuta which is a small Spanish town on the Moroccan coast. Anni

recalls that we arrived in beautiful, dangerous Morocco. At least

now we are in Africa. We entered on the 17th October and left on

the 2nd November. We had to leave because she had trouble

getting an extension on her tourist visa. I think there was some sort of diplomatic friction between Morocco and Germany at the time. Ceuta was duty free and I bought a divers knife for protection. I also had a nylon string guitar with me that I had bought in London. We travelled down to Agadir and took the bus to Marrakech. I can vividly remember travelling through the night on these busses and the local women all shrouded. The police checks where they had spikes laid across the road. I think there was an Arab Summit going on somewhere, there were a lot of police around. At one stop a motorcycle cop got on, looked at my passport and said *"what's your name mister?"* The wayside bus stops with shops selling drinks and supplies. It was always weird arriving at places like Marrakech in the early hours. Usually there were fellow travelers who had some idea about hotels or places to stay or local kids would come and ask if you wanted "room". We were OK for money as we had our wages from the grape picking and stayed in a hotel called Zagora that overlooked the Koutoubia Mosque. We met a very nice English couple where the guy was a juggler and the girl was a dancer. A Moroccan gentleman showed us around the town in a carriage. We also visited other places and I think eventually we took a bus south to go into Africa. This was because Anni's tourist visa was running out and we had to leave the country. When we arrived the boarder was closed due to a conflict in the Spanish Sahara. I remember the town being hot and dusty and there were a couple of Australian guys with a Swedish girl who travelled on the bus down with us. As we were preparing to go north again I noticed they stuck around and talked to them. "Aren't you coming on the bus back?" I inquired, "No mate we're carrying on." This was an unexpected reply. "But the boarder is closed" I tried to emphasize the danger of the situation by nodding towards the troops who were all over the place. "No worries, it will be dark soon, we'll slip over then". He replied with that Aussie self assurance and the girl just looked over and smiled. They seemed happy and obviously had their route planned with no room for detours. Anni and I had already been through some bad experiences with Arabic officialdom where she was shouting at the guy because he would not extend her visa. They could be pretty rough if they wanted and I had to lead her out of there sharpish. In view of that we were not prepared to carry on at the risk of getting turned back with her (by that time) expired visa. If the boarder had not been closed going all the way through would not have been a problem. We would have just made our way back by another route. As things were we decided the best thing was to head back to Spain, and we got back on the bus. Anni recollects that after leaving behind the hardships of Morocco, we stayed in an apartment for 4½ weeks (6th November to 1st December) in a small town called La Carihuela close to Torremolinos. There was sunshine and swimming every day. We adopted a beach dog called Clay who followed us around and guarded the apartment at night. She remembers we had real sadness in our hearts when we said goodbye to him. I seem to recollect Clay running behind the car as we got a lift out of town. There were some small events like stopping in an orange grove to stock up on oranges. Afterwards we got a long ride to Avignon in France. As we continued our journey we stayed in a really nice medieval hilltop village called Mirmande. Back then it was a pretty amazing place. It seemed mostly deserted and we stayed in an empty hostel. The town was like travelling back in time. It was truly beautiful surrounded by forests. I walked in the woods one day and as I rounded a corner there was a dead boar lying across the path that a hunter had shot. We met another English guy at the hostel who was reading Catch 22 by Joseph Heller. After that we stayed in Belfort for 6 days. Then on the 22nd of December we reached Crailsheim and our interesting trip was over. Anni went to Schwab Gmund to her parents for Xmas. I got a lift with a truck back to our apartment in Berlin. Next summer we started our last trip together that ended with me in Canada and her returning to her studies in Berlin where she eventually fell in love with a fellow student. When I look back almost 40 years I think we both walked into everything with heads raised.　　　 I could not have asked for a better companion and our time together, those two short years stayed with me for the rest of my life.

10. The Last Trip (Canada)

Anni recollects that on 27.5.1975 we set out with our rucksacks loaded with a tent, sleeping bags and provisions for a long trip we headed for Fredrikshavn in Denmark and headed for the island of Læsø. She recalls that there was snow and slush and we camped in a farmer's field for 2 weeks eating mussels, fresh eggs and warm milk. One day a group on holiday from the kindergarten in Christiania (at that time known as the free Hippie City inside Copenhagen) came to camp in our field. We had a long talk with them and they were surprised we did not know any of the international news what was going on in the world. I was reading the book 'Big Sur' at the time by Jack Kerouac. It contained his poem "Sea: Sounds of the Pacific Ocean at Big Sur" which I thought was pretty weird at the time. We had an open fire to make coffee and lots of supplies from Berlin like tinned Camembert cheese from Albrecht supermarket. We took a bike trip round the island one day and the weather was really hot and my legs got badly burned. I saw a doctor and I remember that the people on that island were very friendly. Then we moved on to Norway, made a camp by a lake in the woods and stayed there living mainly on trout that we caught or the local boys gave us. I built a raft and made a bath out of big rocks at the edge of the lake while my girlfriend lay around reading in her bikini. After three weeks we moved on. We got a ride with a Canadian couple in a dormobile. We stayed with them for a few days fishing together and exploring the nature. One night round the fire they offered us two return tickets to Canada with about ten days left before they ran out. Anni's school started in August so she did not want to go but I had no job prospects and decided it would be a good idea if I went. Another thing was I had always dreamed of owning a Martin guitar and they were cheaper over there. It was a race against time. We went to Bergen and tried to get passage on a merchant ship but no dice. We ended up taking a ferry to Amsterdam, then onward to England. I don't really remember the sequence of events after that. I must have thought going to Canada was a pretty big step because I went down to Camberley to say goodbye to my folks. Then I went up to Bury St. Edmunds where my grandfather was with relatives to say goodbye to him. I seem to remember Paddy seeing me off on the bus at Frimley. He had a special walking stick with a hollow handle. Then I must have met Anni in London where we spent the last night together at a bed and breakfast near Victoria station. The next day my plane was leaving and we said goodbye at Victoria Station. I landed OK in Quebec and got held up by the customs for a long time. They could not quite grasp my intentions (neither could I). I stayed with the Canadian couple's family in Quebec for a few days. I had to go to the immigration for a visa. One incident I remember was while I was waiting I got talking to an English guy. On his way home he had just left his car at Heathrow Airport and got on a plane to Canada. He had not said anything and left behind a wife and kids! After Quebec I hitchhiked to Toronto where I bought a western guitar made by Gunn. People really stared at me when I walked around with this big box with Gunn written on it. In Toronto I stayed with a lesbian couple who were friends of Anni's. They were really nice and we spent a lot of time clubbing in the city. They had a tape of Buffalo Springfield "Retrospective" that I played a lot. I laid a carpet for them that they had bought but not installed before I left for Vancouver. I was not really into the life in Toronto and everyone said it was more relaxed out on the West Coast. So I set off across the Trans Canada Highway almost the distance from England to Canada. I did eventually buy the Martin guitar in a pawn shop in Victoria before I came back to Europe in 1976. I met a musician over there called Dave who wanted to come to Europe. We ended up in Copenhagen playing in clubs and doing odd jobs. It was a pretty bohemian lifestyle. Then I met my future wife in 1979 got married and raised a family. That is really the end of the story. From then on I just worked in different jobs for decades not months and I never went on the road again.

I end with a letter I sent from Canada to Anni in Berlin. I think it captures where I was at and shows some of the spirit of being on the road. It is undated but sent in the summer of 1975 from Knowles Motel, 2 Miles East on Trans Canada Highway, Moose

Jaw, Saskatchewan, Canada.

I wrote an address to reply to: Youth hostel, 520 Seymour Street, Vancouver, Canada.   *Dear Annie, Hope all is fine. I miss you like crazy and can't find a cure. I hope by next week I can reach Vancouver and find a job fruit picking, so I can fly back to you. I just pine like a dog whose lost his friend. Nothing in this place excites me, I see nothing in everything its very dog eat dog. I can understand why people who immigrate to Canada go home. More money isn't everything coming here wasn't such a mistake. I would never have realized how sick it really is if I hadn't seen it. Got drunk last night haven't had a drink for days. Hopped a train 500 miles it was really nice it was midnight we were camping by a train line these 2 French Canadian guys and a yank. We saw the train stop and ran about a mile down the track then found an empty car, threw all our bags in and it started to move. We all got on and were lying on the floor gasping for breath and laughing, no-one had done it before it was a new experience. We sat with our legs hanging out smoking and there were thousands of stars. We had all been hiking all day and we were ready to do anything. But we got busted the next day by a cop and he took out his gun and we had to sit on our hands and knees and it was pretty ugly so no-one's into trains for a while. So we took this motel and bought a load of beer and it's early in the morning now and people are snoring and its cloudy outside. The floor looks like a battleground rucksacks everywhere, wet clothes hanging like curtains on every wall. I crawled up a couple of hours ago had a glass of Andrews. Had a really full bath then a shower. Wrote a card to Christian and now I 'am writing to you with this letter is a special card just for Annie. I am gonna mix some lemonade, there's nothing else left, we ate everything in sight when we crawled in last night, then played cards. Now all I can see is the pen and all I hear is the occasional car on the highway and all I think about is the person I am writing this to. But I find it very hard to write and not be able to get answers. It's difficult to know what another person is thinking so far away but don't ever think I am not coming back. I never left in a way, at least I don't feel too far from you. I can't wait till we're lying together looking into each other's eyes, touching each other's cheeks. But if things change you must tell me. You did say you didn't think the relationship would last under a long separation that makes me wonder. I am getting something against women in a funny way, here they are pretty stupid even worse than your friend Jane. Ahh this whole place sucks. Just poured some more lemonade now I'll roll a cigarette. Everyone is still asleep, it's cold and raining outside and there's a feeling of despair in the air, the morning after, aha someone in the corner has come to life and gone back to sleep. They all seem so young one's only 17 and he swopped a pair of field glasses for a diamond ring to give his girl, it's kinda nice, they all come from small towns* but they're really OK. Dave the guy I bin hiking with is Japanese Canadian so he has some kind of culture and he's pretty loose, heads in the right place, plays good guitar. Early morning has turned into 10.30 again the guy in the corner has momentarily awoken and decided to go back to sleep. I'll have to finish this and pack my things, another day. I'll give you the address of the Hostel in Vancouver and you can write me a letter there and I hope I make it there to receive it, so just a letter nothing else in case I don't make it. I will be very happy to hear from you, it means a lot to me, so do you, although I shouldn't be telling you too often. Hell it feels like years since we were together but it won't be for long but it will be good for us to be apart for awhile. But that doesn't mean you don't stay faithful, if I find out when I get back you've been messing around with anyone except pictures of me, I'll , I'll, I don't know what I'll do, probably cry and wish I had died at birth. That's not a threat don't take it the wrongly just miss you and this place is shooting my nerves. You take care of yourself anyway carry your gas gun when you go out, really do it. We are living at a bad time, human fellowship has died. Over here they try to disguise it but they can't, people don't trust each other here. There's a big gap between them and no-one's invented anything they can buy to build a bridge across it. We must move to the country, sometime city life will kill us all at a very young age. I'll write again soon. Big kiss, LOTS OF BIG KISSES XXXXXX Love Stephen.

11. Appendix

After reading this I felt it was necessary to add an appendix. Just a few topics that help the reader put more things into perspective. I wrote a few things about the music I liked. Some of influences that were around as I grew up and a final summary.

<u>Some music from along the way</u>

The film director Martin Scorsese says we all have a soundtrack to our lives. In my personal soundtrack Neil Young plays a major part. His music has accompanied me along the road of life. It's an integral part of the theme music to my journey and always has been. I bought the first Buffalo Springfield album when I was 15 from a stall in Petticoat Lane. Actually I walked off with it, I got pushed further and further back in the crowd then some American girl looked at me and gave me a warm knowing smile and I put it inside my jacket and left. I think the stall was illegal but that is no justification. We all like to paint a rosy picture of the past and make ourselves look good. Well, in this case it was not my intention to be a bad boy, the girl encouraged me. I should have been harder, more resolute, and not so easily led astray. The ill-gotten gains or album in question was the first Buffalo Springfield mono version on Atlantic with the wrong track listing. Later I got Neil Young's first solo album in a collection of records I bought from my mate Pip who needed cash to leave home. More detrimental gains as his mum was really upset when he was gone and could not understand where he had gotten the money. Later I got "After the Goldrush" and "4 Way Street". The Buffalo Springfield was quite obscure but the other two albums were well known in the late 1960s and early 1970s. When I went on the road Heart of Gold was released as a single from the album Harvest. That album was Neil's bestseller, four million copies in the States and almost three million in Europe. It was constantly on the airwaves. On certain occasions Neil Young has been able to make time stand still and give me a kind of spiritual fulfillment. Alone in a foreign environment near the South of France in some obscure dusty town, that had a railroad going through a mountain pass. I was standing rucksack on my back, in a bank queue waiting to change money. Suddenly 'Country Girl' came over the speakers and for that moment all was well in the world. Stopping now to recollect that moment I realize I can't really explain it with words. Suffice to say that for those few minutes while my mind wandered nothing else really mattered. Then about 15 years later in a wood in Northern Ontario we had taken a day trip out of Toronto to look at my friend's brother- in- laws house under construction. It was situated on a granite slope surrounded by pine trees that went down to a lake. The house had no walls only the roof was finished. He had these giant speakers and put 'Down by the River' on the stereo. The sound of the music rolled like gentle thunder down through the trees. Time stood still, talk about music fitting the scenery, it was a very moving moment. We all just stood there taking it in. David Crosby really hit the nail on the head when he said Neil Young is a force of nature.

 These songs and others have become like markers in my life. They meant a lot to me during my formative years and still have relevance to me now. What I mean by giving these examples from my life's soundtrack is that they enable me to extract these two moments of listening to Neil Young's music and for a fleeting moment recapture the mood of that moment. I am most certainly not alone in having these moments and I believe this is one of the factors of Neil Young's longevity as an artist. This guy has made many people happy and thereby contributed to humanity through his music. As Yehudi Menuhin once said something along the lines of *"music is a celebration of life it does not lie."*

The Americans I met along the way

I wanted to say more about the Americans and how they influenced me and other people in the UK in the 1960's. They seemed to have a built- in disregard for authority. Even when you see newsreels of how relaxed American G.I.´s were in WW2 or American ground crews sitting on Thunderbolt wings as they taxi round an English airfield. English ground crews would have been crucified for doing something like that but the yanks took it all in their stride. I remember an incident when I was on the road in Torino. It was about five in the morning; I had been up all night and was just wandering around. When suddenly this dark blue American car with golden stars painted on it came haring down the street. It went round the roundabout and stopped in front of me. A guy who looked like Frank Zappa dressed in dark velvet trousers with stars on jumped out and came over. "*Do you know any decent places we can eat man?*" I was a bit stunned and answered "*no man I don't usually eat in restaurants*" he looked at me sideways, nodded and said "*I can dig it man,*" hopped back in the car and hared off. Probably saying to his mates "*boy was that guy ever weird.*" A lightning jolt in my reality, delivered in true American style.

I found that Americans had a hardness and violent reaction to injustice that I as a working class lad did not have. Despite the fact I had endured the slave labour conditions of factory life. Working for real swine that sometimes did not pay my bonuses saying I worked too fast. Even after this I was still left with an ingrown caution towards authority that I found most yanks did not have. I would rather hold my peace, get what I wanted from the situation and walk away. People like Dave, 'bless him,' would have none of that. People rubbed him up the wrong way he was right there. I guess guys like him had to carry knives because one day something will catch up with them. People like me only had them in the rucksack to cut food. To illustrate the point, one evening Dave and I were cruising round in Portofino and he needed the John. So he went into a hotel and politely asked. I stayed outside this fine establishment with a coat of arms on the doormat and smoked a cigarette. He came out infuriated at being refused the use of the bog. I suggested going somewhere else and asking. But Dave was having none of it, he was livid. He found a piece of cardboard and had a crap on it in the car park. Then we walked up to the entrance turned it over on the mat and stamped it in. He had a very clear definition about what injustice meant to him. I had to back him up because I was his mate. This does not mean I would have gone along with anything; if he had said *"they refused to let me use the toilet, I 'm gonna cut his face."* I would have drawn the line and pointed out to him that his reaction was a bit extreme. But a pile a shit never hurt anyone; hell, cleaning that up probably broke the monotony of their night shift! I'll bet they even thanked us in the end. I can still see them looking down at it as we ran away laughing.

The counter culture fought very hard in the US as indeed they did in France (Paris student riots) and Germany (Berlin student riots). But somehow in England it never got that extreme. I took part in CND marches in London and later took part in a demonstration at the funeral of Ulrike Meinhoff in Berlin. But I have never believed in the use of force. I only went on the demo in Berlin because my girlfriend insisted on going because she saw it as necessary and my mate Dave from Canada wanted to go. Next minute I am walking down the street with 15,000 people arms linked and the coppers trying to break us up into smaller groups. It is surprising that the English youth were so conditioned. Maybe because they had won the war, their elders were not as disgruntled as their counterparts on the continent. Because growing up when I did we were very much under the influence of WW2, not only through films but also personal recollections.

Old Soldiers

Like almost every boy growing up in the UK during the sixties I was influenced by males who had been through the war. Especially as I was going through my early teenage years, I would hear stories of events that happened during the last war. But somehow these stories did not complement what I was seeing in magazines. The pictures of Police brutality during the Paris student riots, police beating students with batons as they lay on stretchers being carried into hospitals. This was 1968 and I was 14. These images made a profound impression on me, and I reached the conclusion the world was not as it should be. The police who should be representing the protectors of the people were behaving like savage animals. In 1969 Life Magazine showed pictures of the Mylai massacre, roads littered with bodies of women and babies.

A sequence of photographs; civilians begging for their lives in one picture, then lying dead in heap in the next picture. It was horrendous and these were Americans our allies??? My teachers back then could give no explanation when I asked "How can this be?" All around were memories of war, people would talk of war experiences. Teachers who had seen jungle service would suffer relapses of malaria. I remember vividly a gardener talking about some of the worst things he saw as a soldier in the 8th Army in the desert, the truck in front of him blew up killing everyone. They always followed the tracks in the sand of the previous convey. In this case the Afrika Korps had laid a piece of corrugated iron with sand on and wheel tracks over some mines in the road. He then served in Europe during the invasion of Germany and said the worst thing he saw there was after they captured two young Hitlerjugend. One was about 14 and the other around 12. They were willing to talk and the officer was calling in for a translator. There were some Spanish mercenaries attached to his unit and they were watching them. One of the kids took a step forward, or just moved his foot and the Spaniards sprayed them with machinegun fire. They fell forward screaming with their guts coming out. It was the most terrible thing he saw during the whole war; he said it was just plain murder.

Later in my life I might have found factory life hard but I can't write about the hardship and depravity of it all without thinking

about the blokes I worked with. They had been put through a war
that had also deprived them of their youth. If they read something
about how hard I thought factory life was , the fags would drop
out of their mouths in amazement. They told stories in the tea
breaks of jumping in foxholes under fire only to find a dead
German soldier propped up in there, staring at them. They got out
sharpish because "Jerry was always booby-trapping corpses".
The foreman I had at Frimley Park when I worked as a gardener
was called Bob. He had been a sergeant in the army and served on
the convoys to Russia on the AA guns. It was so cold that he asked
for a transfer and got sent to Singapore that later fell to the
Japanese. He ended up on the Burma Siam Railroad. Only a skin
graft made by the doctor who was also in 'The World at War'
series saved his life. He had no time for colleagues who talked
about guarding Japanese war criminals. He used to sit in the tea
break glowering at them while they talked about how tough it
was. On the way out he would comment *"no war criminals in our
camp, we hung every Japanese soldier we could get our hands on
for six weeks, even the drivers they sent up with food supplies for
us."* So my hardships were maybe small compared to theirs and
my generation was the first one not to have to suffer the
deprivation of war. BUT it was still bloody awful and factory work
was bloody soul destroying. Looking back now I almost think that
each stage of my life prepared me for the next one. Because I had

worked in a factory I knew what hard work was and how to work. That meant wherever I went I could always hold jobs. I had a work ethic instilled in me. I went on the road with Barry, and then moved to London. Living in London prepared me for Berlin which was a tough city back then. The experience of living in Berlin prepared me for Canada. I do not think I would have managed so well in Canada if I had moved there directly from London.

A final summary

Frank Zappa once said something along the lines of *if you now have a very boring life because you listened to your parents and people in authority telling you how to live your life. Well then, you only have yourself to blame for your present situation and you deserve it.* I guess what he means by that is; you only have yourself to blame for the choices you make in your life. In some aspects of this I agree with him. However there is another side where many people are born to privilege and many are not. It is all very well to say; you have to accept your lot and live with it. We are of course all responsible for our future. But for many young people in a class driven society the dice can be very loaded. In my view one of the important things is to have a plan. It is not a necessity but I would advise it. Me and Barry saved up for our trip and worked towards it. Like Barry pointed out we had no return tickets so we were headed where the journey took us. I made a few contingency plans; as this was pre EU days as far as the UK was concerned I took out a medical insurance. At that time the maximum was for three months so I set the start date for three months after we left. I figured we were in for the long haul and if my health deteriorated it would hopefully happen after at least three months. The other thing was we knew each other well and enjoyed each other's company and watched out for each other. He was someone I could trust and depend on. The other thing was luck I guess, things worked out for us. Barry recalls a trip he made later with Paddy to Morocco. There Paddy had his passport stolen and they were robbed all in the first few days. If that had been us in France our trip would have probably ended right there. Luck played a big part in what we did and what happened to us. It had a lot to do with being in the right place at the right time. For example if that car I hitched a ride in had gone to Kaiserslautern and not Berlin, I might have ended up a squaddie[57]. Hopefully your journey through life will be long and you will get time along the way to take stock of things and update your plan!

When I look back now on my youth and that period 'On the Road', I think for that brief period we were truly free. In the way you can only be when you are that young. We had nothing to go back to or for, we could go wherever we wanted and stay as long as we liked. We were living by what was known as 'Hippy ideals' and

---

[57] Slang expression for soldier.

shared what we had. Of course we knew the money would run out some time and we would probably go back to England and find a job (as we both eventually did). But for me it was only temporary, I saved up and left again and never returned.

As for my kids I would not want them to go on the road and all things considered they don't have to. I hope they find all the opportunities they want in life. I have always tried to support them in whatever they choose to do and so far it has all been their own choices. But I understand the kid whose life is going nowhere and he decides to do it. There are some parallels with young people going on the road today who call it a Gap Year. They usually follow a well-trodden path through Thailand and down to New Zealand and Australia. Equipped with mobile phones and the internet social media they can stay attached to the herd. Apart from the fact they usually have return tickets and plan to study the following year, they do many of the things me and Barry did. They stay in Youth Hostels make connections, go to beach parties and create networks and have fun. For me this is one of the key elements of youth, it should be enjoyable, you should be able to look back with happy memories of the things you did and the people you met.

Listen to the Pink Floyd intro to 'Crazy Diamond'[58] when he sings about remembering his youth and you can hear the semi-maniacal cackle of laughter in the background.

That is the kind of feeling I mean.
As for the period when this diary was written, all I can say is.

The sixties were a crazy time. Maybe we were just lucky to be growing up then, where being young made you a part of something. Whatever that something was, we all got off listening to the great music that was around. Having profound life shaking experiences while a sea of change washed through our lives! Maybe that statement is not entirely true but the world in 1973 and the world in 2013 are two very different places and for better or for worse; I was a child of that time.

---

[58] LP. Wish You Were Here © Pink Floyd 1975

ABOUT THE AUTHOR

Stephen M. Catchpole was born within the sound of the Bow Bells.
He grew up in Camberley, Surrey. He went on the road in 1972 and during
the next four years travelled extensively in Europe, North Africa and
Canada. He made a living on the road playing music in clubs and working in
construction. He has an MA in Social Studies from University of North
London and a Cand.mag in History from the University of Copenhagen.
He works as a teacher and has two sons.

www.ingramcontent.com/pod-product-compliance
Lightning Source LLC
Chambersburg PA
CBHW021134020426
42331CB00005B/774